The Square Root of God

ALSO BY TIMOTHY CARSON

Liminal Reality and Transformational Power

Your Calling as a Christian

Six Doors to the Seventh Dimension

The Square Root of God

Mathematical Metaphors and Spiritual Tangents

Timothy Carson

WIPF & STOCK · Eugene, Oregon

THE SQUARE ROOT OF GOD
Mathematical Metaphors and Spiritual Tangents

Resource Publications
An Imprint of Wipf and Stock Publishers
199 W. 8th Ave., Suite 3
Eugene, OR 97401

www.wipfandstock.com

ISBN 13: 978-1-4982-0166-7

Manufactured in the U.S.A.   11/14/2014

Dedicated to the people of
Broadway Christian Church
Columbia, Missouri
A rare and delightful community of the spirit

CONTENTS

Acknowledgments

THIS BOOK WOULD HAVE been impossible were it not for the insights of mathematicians, which mostly elude me and the perspectives of theologians and philosophers that routinely dwarf my own. I have found it gratifying to stand in a rare and sometimes muddy trench between the two. Though some are known to me personally, many more are strangers to me and I to them. I carry such deep appreciation for them all. Any false assumptions that form erroneous conclusions belong to me alone.

What I lack in editorial skills has been compensated for through the exacting copy editing of Nancy Miller. She knows her art and makes me look like a better writer than I really am. And then there were the many subtle words of encouragement from friends, family, and peers who insisted I keep at it. There is nothing quite like the encouragement of friends to steel us against our own doubt.

My greatest hope is that these words will spark in someone, somewhere, a new glimmer of understanding, awareness, and insight. If they do, I will feel as though the adventure was worth it. All other outcomes are left where they belong, with the One who is the square of Itself.

Introduction

We have seen the highest circle of spiraling powers.
We have named this circle God.
We might have given it any other name we wished:
Abyss, Mystery, Absolute Darkness, Absolute Light,
Matter, Spirit, Ultimate Hope, Ultimate Despair, Silence.

—NIKOS KAZANTZAKIS, *THE ROCK GARDEN*

KNOWLEDGE IS LIKE "AN island in a sea of mystery," wrote Chet Raymo. Since the sea of mystery is infinite, the growth of the island of knowledge never depletes it. To the contrary, the more the island's area grows, the more the shoreline's perimeter grows.[1] And as the shoreline's perimeter grows, so grows the interface with mystery. The more we know, the larger the mystery becomes.

The same thing was said differently by the eighteenth century English scientist Joseph Priestley, who drew on images of light and darkness. He said that the greater the circle of light, the greater the boundary of darkness which is created by it.[2]

---

1. Raymo, *When God is Gone Everything Is Holy*, 30.
2. Priestley, *The Theological and Miscellaneous Works*, 25:373.

These particular metaphors depend on categories of geometry. They rely on concepts such as shape, circumference, and area, as well as the contrasts implicit in them. They describe boundaries, edges, and thresholds. But more importantly, as a leap of a different order, they relate mathematical perspectives to a transcendent domain. What is the result? We stumble across a rarified intersection where the sacred and mathematical converge. And what we may discover is just how much light they shed on one another.

Of course, it wouldn't be the first time people insisted that these two worlds belong together. Thinkers from every world civilization throughout history have somehow connected mystical spirituality and mathematics in order to seek truth, to express some comprehensive notion of the universe. Mathematical and spiritual truth have found common expression in cultural sources as disparate as classical Greek philosophy, Egyptian cosmology, the architectural logic of Islamic mosques, the complexity and simplicity of Buddhist temples, metric patterns embedded in Indian ragas, the proportionality of Christian gothic cathedrals, and numerology in the Jewish Kabbalah.

Why has this relationship between mathematics and spirituality been so ubiquitous? A good case can be made that these threads have been woven into the same seamless fabric from the beginning.

How do we understand the dimensions of a black hole, the distance between stars, the behavior of subatomic particles, the finely tuned symmetry of the double helix of DNA, or the veins of a leaf in relation to every other thing? How can we comprehend the relationship between shape, surface, knots, patterns, and braids? What do we make of fractals that replicate their simplicity and complexity in the deep design of every living thing?

All of these complexities hold unities; elegant design appears out of seeming chaos and multiple dimensions. But by what means can we possibly know this multi-faceted reality? What are the limits to our particular modes of knowing? Can we attribute meaning to the data? Does this reality defy logic and reason as understood in ordinary ways? And if we lift the veil, revealing the dynamics that are operative at the micro or macro levels, then what? What stands beyond those?

These questions have been deeply pondered by mathematicians, astronomers, physicists, biologists, philosophers, and theologians through the centuries. In many ways their conclusions have varied as wildly as their beginning points and aims. But more often than many would like to admit, they have ended up pointing in similar directions, finding what the other has already found through different means. And when they provided room for a shared possibility, it often appeared.

As philosopher and physicist Bernard d'Espagnat reminds us, there are veiled aspects beneath what appears to be ordinary reality.[3] What does that mean, *veiled*?

There is, on the one hand, the surface or appearance of reality, and many scientists of the past have preoccupied themselves with that plane. They fall into what might be described as the "realist" or "empiricist" camp. They base what is known on that which is measurable according to ordinary observation. This is the province of everyday physics, the Newtonian universe.

Over and against that position stand the so-called "idealists" who recognize that there is more than that.

The first conviction of idealists is that there is something not meeting the eye that shapes what does meet the eye. Plato is a good example. There are universal essences behind the curtain that shape everything you see in front of the curtain.

The second conviction has to do with the thoroughgoing subjectivity of the one doing the seeing, a subjectivity that participates in shaping the reality of the world. If you swing to the far side of that continuum, you hang by your fingernails with the likes of Jean Paul Sartre and the other existentialists. You are the center of an absurd world that contains no more or less meaning than you provide for it.

How do we know what we know? To begin with, we could go out and play with one of the favorite arguments of physics, *intersubjectivity*. If five people stand on the shore and observe a clipper

3. d'Espagnat, *Veiled Reality*, 367.

ship approaching and describe it in exactly the same way, how the sails are rigged and the way it sits in the water, you would say that the ship has an objective reality. There it is, a thing existing in time and space, attested by multiple sources, several sets of eyes, several brains. This is the kind of argument that helps a positivist sleep like a baby on restless nights.

But using that same clipper ship, let us compare all that supposed objectivity with an apocryphal story often used by Postmoderns. The story has been told that during the colonial period, when clipper ships from Europe first arrived in Mesoamerica, the indigenous people standing on the shore could not see the ships; to them they only appeared as blurs. Their shaman sat on the shore for an extended time until he could "see" the ships, then returned to his people and described what they looked like. Only then could the people return, look, and perceive what they saw.

All this points to just how socially conditioned our sense of reality is; it is a product of the context, experience, and narratives of a particular people. What we observe is filtered in unusual ways by the worldview we already hold, a lens through which we see everything. How much is objective and how much subjective? Are we beholding an objective piece of data or rather a shared idea about what is seen?

If a physicist was walking in the woods, fell down, scraped his knee, and shrieked in pain, but there was no one there to hear the shriek, was there a sound? His voice indeed set off a chain of sound waves that may have rattled tin foil. But those same waves did not strike a human ear drum, travel to the brain, and end up compared to a catalogue of known sounds stored in long-term memory. Something happened but was not experienced, at least by human consciousness. So did it exist?

Most physicists would answer that it most surely did. But do objects and events really exist independently of our awareness of them? Or are things there only because we know them to be there? Since our minds are part of that same reality we observe, do they create reality in the knowing of it?

When we say that reality is *veiled,* we mean that it has a known surface, one that is seen, but has much hiding beneath that surface. It is the surface itself that conceals its contents. We often skate along on this side of the veil without peering behind it.

Take the game of chess, for instance. The contest takes place within the specified boundaries of a square, the pieces assigned abilities to move in different patterns, directions, and distances. All of this takes place in two dimensions, with one notable exception. The Knight is the only piece that can *jump over* other pieces. He has a three dimensional capacity because he is able to move in a plane over and above all the other pieces. If it weren't for the knight, the other chess pieces would have no idea that another dimension even exists. And so it is with reality as we know it: most of the time we move in two dimensions until exceptions or anomalies expose hidden things already at work.

What is true for physics is also true of mathematics. Ludwig Wittgenstein was a philosopher whose work included a huge body of writings devoted to mathematics. Though his perspectives changed over the course of his long career, one of his areas of inquiry stayed constant: the claims that mathematics can and cannot make.

There is a difference, said Wittgenstein, between a mathematical proposition and reality as it actually is. The propositions may resemble reality to a greater or lesser degree, but in each case theory is not entirely equivalent to reality. Mathematics is a human invention, a way that humans have meaningfully arranged and explained the patterns of the world. And those patterns don't exist in the way we know them apart from our effort to describe them. [4]

Considered together, these two philosophers of physics and mathematics shed light on the hidden nature of reality and the limits of any human endeavor to interpret it.

Religious thinkers have also intuited the nature of reality, though in dramatically different terms than their scientific counterparts. Their concepts, mythologies, and cosmologies have surely contrasted with the worldviews of scientists and philosophers, both

---

4. Wittgenstein, *Tractatus Logico-Philosophicus.*

ancient and modern. But their contrasting points of view have hardly been limited with science. They differ among themselves.

Diverse religious cultures have presented the world significantly different perspectives, with almost all of their systems being revised to some degree by religious descendents. In the same way that scientific movements develop particular models that are subject to change, so too are religious traditions reformed, augmented, clarified or abandoned. On that score, science and religion are in the same boat.

The religious search for the absolute, holy, infinite, and divinely ordered cosmos has resulted in a plethora of glimpses into a sacred dimension of life. These inspirations of the human spirit have led to multiple representations in the form of myths, ethical systems, and sacred cosmologies. These traditions typically provide a cosmology and worldview, a unique source of authority such as prophets or seers, a guiding narrative or canon of sacred writings, and an identification of the human predicament along with its solution. In time, these insights and convictions crystallize into fixed systems. And inevitably, much like the old physics or old math, they are self-limiting; the original path of freedom insures its own future obstacles.

Like math and physics, religion is a human activity, a heartfelt response to the mystery of the cosmos. However inspired or lofty, religious expressions of truth are limited by their own finitude. Like math and physics, they resemble reality without being equivalent to it. Our notions of the absolute, the eternal, the all, the nothing, or God do not exhaust that which we attempt to describe. They are *our* notions of God, however inspired or verified by centuries of experience and the testimony of the faithful. They are perceptions, perhaps incredibly helpful ones, but perceptions nonetheless. Every kind of human knowing is shaped by the knower, individually and culturally. And among the body of transcendent knowledge that comes through the spiritual insights of the millennia, and there is much, the most important virtue among them is most surely humility, which is the beginning of wisdom.

Despite the wildly divergent perspectives through which the scientific mind and religious consciousness perceive the universe, parallels continue to emerge. Not the least of these parallels is an array of built-in limits. In this, they sit at the same workbench. And though no one human perspective can possibly exhaust all dimensions of truth, that light has a way of shining through, even when refracted differently through the human prism.

This is a book about that light and that prism. Our starting place is to recognize that every human system is approximate at best. The island has grown, but so has the infinite surface of the unknown. And this is as true for the mathematical domain as for the religious one. What these shared limits provide is a new opening, a possibility, a new dance of engagement. As they both name and veil, we discover a mutually informed new possibility, a whole that is greater than our former sum of the parts.

Transparencies

As we begin this journey, I want to lay my proverbial cards on the table, my philosophical, religious, and world-view assumptions. It is important to know the vantage point of the tour guide. And they are:

God is in everything and everything is in God. This is *not* pantheism—simply equating all things with God, nature = God. More closely, my worldview is similar to *panentheism*, God *in* all things; not equivalent with, but in. This allows for participation, freedom, purpose, creativity, and innovation.

When I say the word *God*, I mean something like the purposeful sacred power that creates and animates the universe. The word does not, for me, represent a supernatural being, even a superlative being among other created beings. It more resembles the singular unfolding and purposeful force that is behind and within the process of the universe. I hope that you will insert whatever word carries that ultimate meaning for you. Your model of the sacred may derive from classical monotheism, but it need not. Indeed, non-theistic traditions should be easily at home here.

Jesus informs my faith in highly significant ways; his reality makes a distinctive claim on me. That claim includes the conviction that his appearance on the world stage was purposeful and revealed the nature of the sacred in his life, teaching, death, and unfolding impact. Because I am a Jesus person, it does not mean that I believe God is inactive everywhere else. To the contrary, Jesus emerged against the backdrop of God's universal presence in all time and space. If you do not share this particular understanding of Jesus, but are searching for spiritual truth in other ways, it is my hope that you will, nevertheless, discover insights that are truly helpful.

I am *not* turning to mathematics to fill a gap, to provide answers absent in faith. Rather, I am drawing upon a human invention that *points* toward deep patterns inherent in the cosmos. This mathematical pointing parallels the pointing of religious symbols. I am not turning to mathematics to provide certainty, but rather to place its pointing alongside other pointing. I am primarily borrowing mathematical concepts in the service of spiritual metaphors, drawing parallels in the language of faith that allow us to travel beneath the surface to what is hidden and unseen And I recognize the limits of mathematical metaphors; like any metaphor, they are inevitably incomplete.

I believe the universe objectively exists apart from our perception of it; it is something real and actual, regardless of the distortion or accuracy of our observation. Though I am not an existentialist, believing that the only meaningful universe is the one we project, I do believe that our subjective perceptions of the universe do contribute to its reality. What exists is granted meaning by the ways one embraces what exists.

I also believe that it is possible for the insights of mystical experience to provide clues to mathematics, since those insights draw on infinite images and concepts not limited by rationalistic and material models. New categories of infinity require models with room for infinity. There is give and take.

As our island of knowledge grows, so does the shoreline of mystery; there is no cause for reserve: To the boats. Cast off the lines and hoist the sails. Out we go to the open sea, under starry skies that are as infinite as the minds and hearts that may comprehend them.

1

The Number 1

THE NUMBER 1 IS usually giddy, delighted in its unity, ecstatic about its own irreducible, undivided self. And not only giddy, but essential. After all, 1 is a factor of every number, included as an indispensable part of all other numbers; it can never be completely factored out of any other number.

Just imagine that rarified status: a unified singularity that is always a component of, a part of everything else, no matter how complex it gets. Now that's an important position, being number 1, because you're the only number that plays a part in every other number just by being yourself. You are totally complete in and of yourself, yet at the same time related to everything else, making everything else possible.

For example, 1 x n (number) = n for every number. No exceptions.

The number 1 is present in every other number, no matter how big or how small. Since there are infinitely many numbers, and number 1 is a part of all numbers, it is not only unity in itself but also infinity through participation in everything else which it makes possible and of which it is a part.

The runner up is the *prime number*. Of course, the number 1 is a prime itself, something that the other primes often choose to overlook. In fact, more than one prime number has become grandiose about its own uniqueness. Containing no dividers other than itself and the number 1, a prime number often looks down upon those half-breed mutts made up of, well, who knows what. Take the number 4. Let's be honest: 4 is nothing more than 2 x 2. What's so unique about that? It's just made up of something else. Now 13, there's a number for you. You can't multiply anything by anything else to get 13, except, of course, 13 x 1.

Prime numbers have been known to look at themselves in the mirror for hours at a time, just beholding their beautiful primeness. Until number 1 waltzes by, that is, smirking as he goes. number 1 always believes that all those grandiose primes have been afflicted with some kind of amnesia, forgetting themselves and their place. They have either forgotten that their identity is all wrapped up with number 1, or else they are full of pride, a refusal to acknowledge their dependence.

Primes are not the only ones with an attitude. Take *Sigma*, a concept used to indicate a sum of all parts, a totality. He thinks he is really big stuff. But that totality is really a composite, a compilation, a conglomerate. Sigma is a defined bag of popcorn. It's a bag of everything added together. If you were Sigma, you might be tempted to brag. But that bragging would be misplaced and short-lived. Number 1 would always be standing in the shadows, reminding you that you are neither more nor less than multiples of number 1. Now that is humbling, and not only for Sigma. It is humbling for every number other than number 1.

And that's why, in the end, the wheel always rotates back to number 1 and its irreducible, undivided unity, the basis of everything else, a singularity that is the simplicity within every complexity, a unity that extends infinitely.

AΩ

The *Shema*, the central prayer from the Jewish prayer book, comes directly from the Biblical commandment to *hear* (Deut 6:4). And what shall be heard? For starters, that the Lord your God is *One*.

On its most basic level, this is the central conviction of monotheism, that there is ultimately one and only one God, not a polytheistic system, not a pantheon of gods. Even Biblical language that reflects a first-person plurality refers to a heavenly court, not numerous deities (Gen 1:26). The essential metaphysical pronouncement is that there is but one ultimate and seamless reality and its source. There is one.

Many polytheistic mythologies do recognize one superior or high god, a first among equals, higher than any others. Some go so far as to create a kind of two-tier system, with the pantheon of second-string gods closer to earth and one higher, absolute, and transcendent, where the theistic buck stops. This is not countenanced in radical monotheism. The others don't exist; not as gods, they don't. Maybe angels, but it stops there.

One of the nuances of Biblical monotheism is that even if you don't believe other lesser gods exist, but your neighbor does, you nevertheless continue to insist that there is one God in relation to your neighbor's gods. You may not believe they exist, but you state that, just in case, as a blanket clause, the one God is one of all. It is stated in the Decalogue this way: *You shall have no other gods before me* (Exod 20:3). What gods? Well, those of my neighbor, the ones I don't believe in. So either way, there is but one God in the field of real or imagined gods.

There are, of course, the idols that masquerade as God, replacements that we treat or honor *as though* they were God. The correlate to not worshipping other gods is not creating or making other gods (Exod 20:4). Our self-created idols are impotent, without the ability to speak or act (Heb 2:18). We only delude ourselves in elevating the relative and contingent to the level of the ultimate (Isa 41:29, Jer 10:5). Anything created by human hands is, by definition, not God. God creates the human creature, but not the other way around (Ps 115:4).

The *Shema*, however, contains another facet that extends the concerns of monotheism to another level. When Israel hears that their God is one, they reserve an exclusive position for God in relationship to real or imagined competitors. But they also believe that the oneness of God speaks to the *indivisibility* of the divine life. God is one in the sense that God is unified and not sub-dividable. God is internally one and not many.

Like the number 1, God is an irreducible and undivided unity, a singularity that is the simplicity behind every complexity. This oneness is the foundational and undivided mystery within the cosmos, the harmony centering human communities, the common thread uniting diverse cultures and nations, and the interior peace of an undivided mind.

Along with the French Jewish sage Rashi, the twelfth century Jewish scholar Maimonides occupies the preeminent place of honor around the table of Jewish thought and practice. His systematic interpretation of the Torah, *Mishneh Torah*, is still standard reading for scholars and yeshiva students today. In addition, his *Guide to the Perplexed* was written in Arabic while he served as the physician to the Sultan in Egypt. It is a commentary on the *Mishneh*.

One of Maimonides' writings, *Thirteen Principles of Faith*, framed what would become a Jewish Credo, a catechism for believers that is often found in Jewish prayer books. The first of those principles recognizes the existence of God, but the second, God's oneness:

> *We believe that this Primal Cause is One. [This oneness] is not like the oneness of a pair, nor like the oneness of a species, nor like man, whose complex oneness may be divided into many units, nor like the oneness of a simple body, which is one in number but may be divided and separated without end. Rather, the Lord (YHWH) is One with a Oneness that knows no parallel in any manner. This is the Second Principle, as affirmed by the verse (Deut 6:4):* "Hear O Israel, God is our Lord, God is One."[1]

---

1. Maimonedes, *Thirteen Principals of Faith*, #2.

In terms of cosmology, the undivided God serves as source and sustainer of all things, the essential creative force behind every force, principle, and pattern in time and space. The one God is the unified formula explaining every other formula, the foundational aspect of every other aspect. The unified God is not explained by other elements but is the explanation for every other element.

In the middle of every Friday night prayer service, the Hasidim recite a passage from the mystical *Zohar*. At the onset of the Sabbath it describes the entrance of the feminine *Shekhina*, the active presence of the sacred. She abides with humble, joyful hearts that invite and await her. But lest we somehow separate and subdivide the Holy, the writer makes it clear that there is but one reality.

> *The Shekhina turns to the mystery of Oneness as He does*
> *In order that One and One would become One.*
> *This is the mystery of "Yahweh is One and God's Name is One."*
> *The mystery of the Sabbath is the Sabbath Herself.*
> *It is Her uniting with the secret of Oneness, of uniqueness,*
> *that She may immerse in the Secret of One.*[2]

The math is counter-intuitive: $1 + 1 = 1$. There is no other possible sum. There may be complexity, what the reading calls uniqueness, but it all belongs to One.

Even that which appears to be chaotic, a masked swirl of seemingly unrelated matter and occurrence, has as its ground the source, origin, and engine of the singularity of God. If the One participates in all, then even chaos has a hidden symmetry, for everything is always and everywhere constitutive of the singularity within it. There is a simplicity on the far side of complexity.[3]

AΩ

Of course, the theological conundrum that has pitted serious monotheists against all comers is the Christian doctrine of the *Trinity*. The word, trinity, is not found in the Christian canon of scriptures. The metaphysical relationship of creator, son, and spirit

2. Schachter-Shalomi, *All Breathing Life Adores Your Name*, 49–50.
3. Whitehead, *The Concept of Nature*.

did not preoccupy the first generation of Christians except as regarded their distinctive roles in the Christian narrative. A solution was not required for a problem that did not yet exist.

As the Jesus of history became more, became the Messiah of faith, early Jewish Christians did not especially need a philosophical explanation. The Messiah was God's Messiah; he belonged to God, was sent by God. That Christians experienced the active presence of God, what they called the Holy Spirit, was not a new idea for Jews who had already named that reality of God in many of their own ways, including that of the *Shekhina*. Even the most esoteric of the canonical Gospels—John—defined Jesus and Spirit not so much in metaphysical terms as through the language of relationship and participation. But that fairly modal understanding of the many ways the one God manifests would soon change.

It was not long before theologians and kings wanted more. They sought a comprehensive conceptual model to explain the interrelating persons of creator, son, and spirit. As much as the bishops wanted to unite the church, Constantine wanted to unite his kingdom. And the end of that story is that Plato took the philosophical day; the council of Nicaea provided Platonic categories to describe the interrelationship between the divine puzzle pieces. The influence of Alexandrian bishop and theologian Athanasius determined the theological outcome. Later, Augustine of Hippo insured its continuance for centuries to come.

If your starting point becomes a metaphysical construct in which the persons of creator, son, and spirit must comprise a unity, then you have to explain just how those entities relate to one another. You must establish the equality of all, distinctiveness, and, when appropriate, which ones occupy subservient positions and how they do so. You must figure out how the son can be divinely co-equal and yet participate fully in humanity. You must explain how the spirit is co-equal and yet dispatched by others of the triumvirate, the creator and son. The Trinity is a concept driven by numbers, acting as a symbol.

Augustine used numerology to explain the Trinity in particular ways. Mostly he drew upon the numerical proportion of 1 to 2.

The proportion of the single to the double, said he, arises from the number 3. $1 + 2 = 3$. That means that all elements added together complete the proportionate formula.

Augustine also used a mathematical sequence in which each new integer added to the sequence contributes to the sum of all that preceded it: $1 + 2 = 3 + 3 = 6$ . . . He then found every way in which the number 6 provides a key to other numerological solutions by extending it and identifying how it is the square root or the square of another number. This mathematical sequence, in addition to Platonic ontological categories, provided the theoretical basis of the Trinity as understood by Augustine. [4]

If we carefully consider the mathematical structure embedded in the language of the *Nicene Creed*, we find something else. The tri-existing aspects of father, son, and spirit are both sequential *and* cumulative: father (1), son begotten by the father (2), and spirit proceeding from the father and son (3): $1 + (1 + 2) + (1 + 2 + 3) =$ Triune God.

The primary conceptual problem with this formula is an inconsistency between its theological and mathematical dimensions. In fact, it has it exactly backwards. If the principle of the indivisibility of God was strictly followed, *the son and spirit would never be added together with the father to equal one God*. Rather, if the creator is unrivaled as indivisible number 1, it can only *add itself to others* to make them what they are. Others exist only because number 1 provides their basis. The correlate to that proposition is true as well: others exist only insofar as they participate in number 1.

That is the theological and mathematical problem. Even though the *Nicene Creed* begins with the unequivocal statement that "We believe in one God," that proposition is not consistent with its math; the Trinity is actually presented as an *aggregate* of three, or to cite the common phrase, *three in one*. What this means, mathematically speaking, is that the historic formulation of the Trinity was equivalent to *Sigma*. And as we know, *Sigma* is the sum of all parts, a composite, a compilation, a conglomerate. When the

4. Augustine, *The Trinity*, 158–59.

Trinity of Nicaea conceptualizes *three in one,* it creates *Sigma* by default, a conglomerate of 1 + 2 + 3.

This is an inescapable problem as regards the number 1. This model of the Trinity adds everything together, all integers included in the final sum. And that is exactly the argument against it— namely, that *God can never be the product of addition.* God is not the product of anything. In fact, the oneness of God does not allow for explanation by any formula like this. Rather, we have the opposite case: *God is the unity, the indivisible number which is a part of every other number.*

As the Hasidic master the Ba'al Shem Tov put it, "No existence has existence other than the self-existence of God."[5] Regardless of multiplicity and multiple forms, there is but one sacred reality.

One of my Rabbi friends once said, "You know, you Christians get your act together in terms of having more than one God and we'll have something to talk about." On that score most Jews and Muslims are united: Christians, in their formulations of the Trinity, occupy precarious theological territory. And when Christians are most receptive, we understand that critique; we become aware of the holes in the traditional formulations. What are friends for?

A Deist like Thomas Jefferson, for instance, insisted that God was one, not many, a contrast to the traditional presentations of the Trinity. In his letters to contemporaries we discover his true point of view. "Skip the fourth-century theologian Athanasius and his Trinitarian smoke and mirrors. You've traded in the God of Jesus for the abracadabra of Plato."[6] The answer for the future, thought Jefferson, was the oneness of God and liberating Jesus from all those, including Biblical writers, who have distorted him and his message. Granted, his perspective was highly influenced by Enlightenment rationalism, but the conviction that God was essentially indivisible and one was hardly unique to him.

How might we think of this differently, preserving the oneness of God as we reinterpret the historic Christian formulations? And how can mathematics and theology inform one another?

5. Schachter-Shalomi. *A Heart Afire,* 34.
6. Gaustad, *Faith of the Founders,* 102.

The formula that successfully expresses the relationship between creator, son, and spirit is something akin to Einstein with a twist. In the same way that his famous equation places energy on one side of the equal sign and everything else on the other, so *God is on one side of the equal sign with the rest of the formulation on the other.* By analogy, that is the way to retain the unity and indivisibility of God. God is on the indivisible left side of the equal sign and everything else is on the right side, and nothing on the right can exist apart from participating in what's on the left. Remember that the number 1 is present in itself and is present in all other infinitely many numbers, and in this sense combines both unity and infinity. In order to combine these two properties of unity and infinity, I am defining a new symbol that includes both: 1∞. That allows what would be an illogical, impossible formula to become quite possible. It might look something like this (1∞ = God, 2 = Son, 3 = Spirit):

$$1\infty = (1\infty + 2) + (1\infty + 3)$$

God is one and God equals everything. And God equals God participating in and being a part of everything else, including the son and the spirit. In the above formula, the son and spirit have been assigned *prime numbers* for a reason; they contain no divisors other than themselves and the number 1. And thinking of the son and spirit as prime numbers, paired only with their indivisible, infinite God, may be the theological and mathematical way to free ourselves from an untenable formula we have felt constrained to defend for too many centuries.

As we see above, this does not detract from either Jesus or the active role the Spirit. To the contrary, it grounds them in God, granting significance to the degree that God is always a part of them.

The more seriously we take the *Shema*, "Hear, O Israel, the Lord our God is One," and the first line of the *Nicene Creed*, "We believe in One God," the better things will go for us.

Like $\sqrt{1} = 1$, so the $\sqrt{God}$ = God always and in every case.

This ancient insistence on the necessity of One may be the antidote for much of the fragmentation of our times. As opposed to dualism, polarization, and the segmenting of life, the Oneness of the reality we name God may provide a transforming vision. Its singular nature unfolds into elegant complexity, finely tuned for life, multiplying into a seamless panorama. What we call God is not a separate reality from the created universe, but rather an embedded orienting principle.

ΑΩ

One day my wife came into my study and told me the doctor just asked her to come back in to talk about some recent tests. In short order we were in the doctor's office as she interpreted some very concerning results. We were in shock. What could this mean? And what were the stakes? We imagined the worst, as much as we tried to think positively.

That first consultation led to specialists, a myriad of diagnostic procedures, and finally a diagnosis. It was not pretty. We were dealing with a potentially life-threatening form of cancer. As much as we called on faith and trust in God, an inevitable fear moved in like a squatter in our back yard. With alarming regularity he knocked at our door and intruded with his simple, powerful entrances. He was real, as real as the disease was.

Fortunately, in Kathy's case, her particular form of cancer was responsive to hormone blockers. This treatment is relatively new among the spectrum of treatments. It meant taking an oral pill once a day. She built up her body and immune system with the right nutrients and vitamins. Moderate exercise became increasingly important. Social support and engagement created a web of relational support. And then there was faith, there was God, the foundation of our lives up until that very moment.

We have lived through crisis before, and our trust in God has always played a central, orienting role. Not only do we lean on the presence of the Spirit for direction and consolation, but our Christian story provides a rudder in choppy seas. What to do? Lots, that's what. We had Christian practices from the ages, prayer and prayer for us by faithful souls far and wide, spiritual meditation that centered the mind in the midst of anxiety, centering images and rituals, communal worship, and the central Christian conviction that one of the keys to spiritual liberation is to focus outside of ourselves when we are most tempted to cave in on ourselves. Just look around, find the testimony of the saints, share the experience of those who have been through it before, and start praying for and reaching out to others who are also suffering.

Somewhere in the midst of all this we had an epiphany. It had to do with the relationship between religion and science. More specifically, our awakening had to do with God and modern medicine.

We have never been dualists, separating out God and medicine as though opposites, as if medicine was some fall back for a lack of faith in God's healing power. We had always embraced both as gifts—the mystery of God's healing presence in our lives and the blessing of the medical arts. But what our up-close experience did was to refocus our understanding of God's province even more.

So often you hear people expressing their support for you something like this: "We're going to pray for a mighty miracle of healing, placing you in God's care, praying for God's will to be done, that you have all the presence and patience you need. And, of course, we hope the doctors do their best, too." Those are actually wonderful sentiments. They are lifting us up to God and at the same time wishing us success with the medicine. It's not that it's wrong, because it's not. The idea just doesn't go far enough.

If we were to express this mathematically, the popular concept is something like this:

$$(God = 1\infty, Medicine = 2):$$
$$1\infty \text{ and/or } 2 = Healing \text{ and } Wholeness$$

The problem with this is twofold. The first is making God optional, the unnecessary integer if medicine is successful. That means that the more medicine discovers, the more God shrinks in relevancy. That is an inadequate view of God in the world.

The second problem is the way that medicine is related to the God part. This way of thinking has it backwards. It parallels the problem with the trinity in which God is added to things to make God. If God is One, that's not the way to understand it. We need to turn the equation around and make sure that God equals everything and everything equals God:

$$1\infty = (1\infty + \text{Healing}) + (1\infty + \text{Medicine})$$

God is one and God equals everything else, including what we might call spiritual healing and also healing through medicine. When we got that, we began to make a dramatic change in our thinking, in our language, and where we placed God in the whole healing process.

We first began with our language. Now we talk about God's doctors, God's medicines, God's research, God's healers, and God's healing centers (hospitals). It all belongs to God. In fact, God is participating in it all. There is nothing in which God is not a factor. Every treatment is a blessing. Each and every healing center staff person is an agent of God, whether they know it or not.

Suddenly the relationship with prayer, spiritual centering, the mind-body-spirit connection, harmony between brain and soul all came together. All is One. They are seamless, all comprised of the same divine energy that manifests itself differently.

The formula also makes it clear that modern medicine is not equivalent to God. To the contrary, God includes medicine as part of the unfolding life of God. This parallels the relationship between God and the created world, God and nature. God is not merely equivalent to the natural order (pantheism), but rather is the *source of and participates in* the created order (panentheism). The same is true of God and medicine. And getting that relationship right makes all the difference.

When it came to prayer, we were set free from even an unconscious dualism between prayer and medicine. With God as One we fully embraced a holistic understanding of praying for healing. Our prayers, the prayers of many, were not over and against what was happening down the street in the clinic. Rather, God *was* down the street in the clinic. That set us free to be multipliers of grace, to seek the power of the spirit to lift and overcome, to cast out and gather together, fill and leave no room for that which is not God.

In the roller coaster ride of life-threatening illness, saying those things is much easier than doing them. The journey of healing in God is full of twists and turns, and our human frailty makes frequent cameo appearances. We truly come to know our need of God. And God, in all God's manifestations, becomes more and more real as we exclaim with the Psalmist that the earth is the Lord's and the fullness thereof (Ps 24:1).

This is all confirmed by the finely tuned mechanisms of life. In the impossibly complex spiral staircase of DNA, the delivery system of the genetic codes that determine and replicate life, there exists the deepest simplicity and unity. We humans are, genetically speaking, 99.9% the same. We even share an incredible genetic commonality with plants. This only reminds us that, at the bottom of life's complex operating system, it's all one.

That includes everything, of course, because God is one, unified and infinite. And the $\sqrt{\text{God}}$ = God every time.

2

Circle Up

EVERY RESPECTABLE CIRCLE KNOWS that it could never exist without its center. The center is the indispensable essential to which everything else is oriented. Every point on the circumference of a circle is exactly the same distance from the center as every other point. What that means is that every point on the circumference, though occupying a distinct position, is an equal peer to every other point beside it. All of this is so because of the identical relationship every point shares with the center.

Imagine a group of ten drummers evenly positioned around the one large ceremonial drum, each holding a beater in his or her hand. Each person is a different age and comes from a different walk of life. Some are more experienced at drumming than others. As each player attempts to strike the drum head in rhythm and with the same force as all the others, the strike is, in actuality, slightly harder or softer, a millisecond sooner or later than those to his right or left. Though the total effect sounds like unison, what we are really hearing is a sonic illusion. Listeners combine all of these closely related sounds and merge them into one experience, a gestalt, one perceived sound.

What the people in this musical ritual share, in addition to their culture, tradition, and a sense of acting in concert, is a relationship to a center. The physical center is the drum. But that physical center is representative of an even more important invisible, symbolic center. Each person on the circumference may in fact be quite unique, but this uniqueness in no way changes the determining relationship to the center. That relationship to the center becomes neither stronger nor weaker due to factors such as hair style, beater timing or volume. Each person remains in exactly the same relationship to the center as any other. All points on the circumference of a circle share exactly the same relationship to the center.

ΑΩ

But what if several points exist in greater or lesser distance from the center? How is the relationship different among points that exist on concentric circles, those circumferences set at different distances from the center? Our solar system might be a case in point.

The planets of our solar system circle the sun as the result of its gravitational field. Their orbits are not pure circles, of course, but rather large elliptical patterns. They all engage in their orbits at different distances from the sun, their center, by virtue of the relative mass of each and the gravitational force of the sun. From planets to stars, galaxies to atoms, matter and its energy are oriented to and shaped by the centers that hold them.

Concentric circles share the same center. By solar comparison, Mercury and Venus are both in relationship to the same sun. The star around which they orbit holds both of them in the same gravitational field. In that relationship they are identical. They differ, however, according to their relative distance from the center, a distinction that alters the intensity of realized force. But gravity isn't the only factor relating to distance and intensity. Other forces and constants are in play, such as light.

Because the two planets occupy different distances from the sun, the intensity of light varies for each according to that distance. That difference in intensity translates to a wide variance between the surface temperatures of those planets. And those differences in temperature are determinative as regards the flourishing of life.

The different location of points on two or more concentric circles does not change their primary relationship to the center, but it does change the intensity and quality of the relationship. And there are infinitely many concentric circles, all defined by varying lengths of each radius.

To use a familial example, the two sons of the classic Prodigal Son parable of Jesus (Luke 15:11–32) shared the same father but grew into two separate orbits. The younger son abandoned home and family, and spun out and away from the source of life. That relocation resulted in very different consequences, very different trajectories. In fact, the two sons moved to such different circles that they became estranged and unmindful of one another. The happy surprise of the parable, though, is that this variance in the degree of intensity never interrupted the primary love of the waiting father. His gravitational field, so to speak, continued to exert influence for both, though in changing degrees of intensity. His position and radiance remained constant though the relative position of his sons changed.

In the Christian tradition, this is one of the Biblical stories that speaks of the reality of *grace*. The boys ended up in very different places, very different orbits, but that distinction could never change the fact that they were related to the same father. In fact, the father loved both in their particular circumstances. No matter how far the younger son fled that gravitational pull, the primary relationship was never severed.

This truth was the source of great suffering for the elder son, who stayed close to his father's side throughout the years. He could not understand how his brother's tenuous relationship with his father, his diminished intensity, would not rupture the bonds they shared. The elder brother believed that the great distance of the younger son from his father would spell the end of love. He could not comprehend the difference between the primary forces of a relationship and degrees of intensity within that relationship. It perplexed him that the father's love remained constant. When the younger son finally came to his senses, returned and thereby changed his proximity to the center, the intensity of relationship increased. As father and younger son embraced one another, it was as though he had never left in the first place, though of course he had and knew it. That's grace.

If there is a way to understand how different people are located differently in relationship to their source, their creator, this is it: as points are located differently on concentric circles they have different degrees of intensity in relation to the center, though they remain related to that same center.

That awareness is what allows people of faith to say without contradiction, "This person may not love God now, but that does not diminish God's love for them." Or, in the same way, when people lose mental acuity due to accident, aging, or disease, a loss that might erase memory and their ability recognize those closest to them, that does not mean they are loved any less for it. To the contrary, those around them may love more than ever before, a great compensation for the diminished capacity of the beloved. We may not know, but we are known. We may not remember, but we are remembered.

Similarly, though we may not know God, or love God, or surrender to God, we are known by God, loved by God, and remain sought out by God. Intensity changes, depending on how far the planet is from the sun, but the fundamental relationship does not change. Grace abides as the father waits. In fact, that is the divine nature: the sacred knot will never untie no matter how far that child travels away. The speed of light is constant and takes longer to travel to its destination the farther away it is. At greater distance its intensity is more diffused. But it does arrive after all.

ΑΩ

Circles are built into the structure of the universe in countless ways. From trees and their growth rings to the way that water forms into round pools, circles are everywhere. From the beginning of human time thoughtful persons have represented the cycle of seasons through stone circles and Aztec calendars. The daily rhythm of hours and minutes is represented around the circular clock face.

When a child takes a stick and draws a circle in the dirt, what intuition traces the pattern? Is this simply mimicking other circles seen in nature, like the shape of the full moon on a clear night or gazing into a mother's face during infancy? Did the nomads of central Asia create their circular yurt dwellings as a result of simple physics, the structure that best exhibits strength against the raging wind? Beyond the deep patterns of nature or the way humans have employed circles in practical ways, how has the circle emerged as the geometric shape laden with more universal symbolism than perhaps any other?

The circle has become, symbolically speaking, the shape that best expresses social unity, metaphysical harmony, cosmic balance, and interpersonal wholeness. Harmonious community and spiritual solidarity have often been expressed through circles. The Pueblo tribes of the Southwest expressed unity through their sacred meeting areas, the subterranean circular *Kivas*. The five Olympian rings interlock to symbolize international solidarity, circles with circles, unity within unities. Mythical stories of the Knights of the Round Table carried hope for truly egalitarian relationships of mutual respect and balanced power. Sufi circle dances whirl co-equal partners around the same imagined center and share ecstasy together. And every group that has ever joined hands and sung *Kum Ba Yah* around a campfire did so not only from tradition, but out of experience: when we form a circle, the energy that wraps itself around our perceived center, our source, is like no other. We are at our best in a circle. A center longs for its circle and our circle gathers around our center.

AΩ

Of course, the circle informs our understanding of religious communities. If a community of faith forms a circle around its sacred center, then every member of that circle remains related to the source regardless of their location on any radius. As all beings are related to the divine source, they find themselves nearer or farther by degree at any given moment. Participation, then, is always relative as intensity increases and decreases in relation to distance from the center; the closer one is to the center, the more intense the relationship; and the further away, the weaker and more diffused. Like walking a labyrinth, we alternately move closer to and farther from the center as we circumnavigate it: relationship remains; intensity varies.

That is why belonging in a spiritual community is always related to gravity and distance. If one is in the same orbit as other planets revolving around the same gravitational center, there is an equal sense of relatedness—but with different degrees of intensity. The temperature on Venus is exceedingly greater than on Saturn, though both planets relate to the same sun. What distinguishes them is distance and the resulting intensity or richness of relationship.

In every religious community individuals will always be at different places as regards spiritual formation, commitment, participation, and leadership. The Christian understanding of grace— the unconditional love of God for every created being—insists that we are all related to the source, the same center of the circle. To believe otherwise, that we are somehow qualitatively different than our neighbor, is to stand atop precarious balsa wood stilts. Nonetheless, the degree of trusting faith we exercise—our response to and participation in the gravity of God's radiating love—does places us either nearer or farther from the center at any given moment, thus providing greater or lesser richness.

True community is formed not only because of loyalty between members who form the circumference, but because of their shared fidelity to the same center. That one factor most determines who they are individually and as a community. Their potential for unity is defined most importantly by the center they share, more than, for instance, what they have in common or how much they agree. In the same way that a circle cannot be itself without a center point, so a religious community cannot be itself without an orienting center. Communities that lose a vibrant sense of the center point not only lose their reason for being, but also their resiliency.

Being nice, being friendly, having a great coffee fellowship is not enough. If the center does not hold, the community scatters, like a flock without its shepherd.

Among the great religious traditions, the orienting center is symbolized differently. For Jews, the temple was the center of the Jewish sacred universe, and in the center of the temple the holy of holies. For Christians, Christ is symbolized as the head of the body, the church, the cornerstone of a spiritual house of living stones. Islam defines the pilgrimage to Mecca, the Hajj, with the circumnavigation of the Kaaba, as one of the essentials of the faith. Buddhism turns its practitioners to the eight-fold path, a schema represented by a wheel. Regardless of the tradition, symbolized reality depends on the relationship of a circle to its center.

AΩ

Perhaps the greatest challenge for us today is the realm of interfaith understanding. It is here that the symbolism of the circle holds the greatest potential.

In times ancient and modern, the relationship between the religions has often been characterized as one religion looking out toward others from the perceived vantage point of the center. In this view, with one's own tradition at the center, others either stand outside of ultimate truth or exist only as a weakened version of it. The hallmark of this exclusivist model is its arrogance, presuming absolute truth. In the religious traditions that are designed this way, the world of religions is arranged like a game of musical chairs; when the music stops, some find chairs and others don't.

A universalist model envisions novelty and common destination at the same time. It is the "many paths up the same mountain to a shared summit" relativist schema. This model recognizes distinctiveness among the many paths and they all ultimately end up at the same destination. The arrival, though, is understood irrespective of individual paths. The problem with this model is that it often minimizes the distinction between the different paths that actually have different aims and ends; their systems actually participate in different concentric circles. These different points on different circumferences might not necessarily contradict one another, such as enlightenment in the Buddhist path and salvation in the Christian one, but they do have contrasting notions of history, the purpose of human existence, and the nature of reality itself. A lazy universalism might draw the conclusion that they are all basically the same when it is really more accurate to say that their different paths lead to different mountain tops.

Then there is the assimilation solution: I include you into my religion if you are close enough, virtuous enough, wise enough, and holy enough. On the surface and compared to many other positions, this is kinder and gentler. The admirable impulse is to include. And that is good. The unintentional consequence, however, is making you an extension of me in order to make you acceptable. I make you an anonymous Christian or Jew or Hindu. You don't know it, but you're good enough to be one of us. You're such a hero that I name you a secret Muslim or Baha'i or whatever I happen to be. I define your virtue by how closely you approximate my own religious sensibilities. At its worst, this impulse to include you in me becomes a form of religious colonialism; it presumes that one religion is the measure of all others, that there is an absolute—usually my religion—by which others are measured and to which they would aspire if only they knew better. When they fulfill my religious expectations, then they are at their best. They just think they are on a different circumference when really they inhabit mine.

Of course, on the getting along level, nothing is wrong with large-hearted tolerance, and we would do well to have more of it. Just being kind and loving to the neighbor would be an enormous, positive improvement. But agreeing to disagree and embracing diversity is no substitute for a robust re-envisioning of the place and value of the great faiths in relation to one another.

As we consider the exclusivist, universalist, inclusivist, and tolerance models, we find them all wanting. What is needed is something else, something more. What is needed is the circle.

AΩ

Not too long ago I was driving into a rainstorm with the sun at my back. Because the angle was just right, a double rainbow appeared before me. It comprised two, unbroken half circles that spanned all the way from the left horizon to the right. As I looked at the two great half circles, my imagination completed them so that they became two 360-degree circles. And there at the midpoint of the horizon was the hypothetical center point—always elusive, shifting as I did, moving with my change of position.

Let's assume, for argument's sake, that neither of the rainbows had awareness of the other. Without either rainbow knowing that the other rainbow existed, both rainbows remained, nevertheless, related to the same center, regardless of what distance they might be from that center.

In addition, both rainbows comprised exactly the same light that contains the entire spectrum of color. They shared that without knowledge of the other. That color spectrum extends in two directions at the same time, reaching beyond the place where we can see it. If a double rainbow provides two full color spectrums side by side, both of which extend in two directions at once, that means that eventually the two spectrums will cross one another, blend and intertwine. Both arcs share the same properties in the same space and time. Does one arc simply stop where the other starts? No, they are both complete, the surface of their reflection received differently by the eye. They continue to orient themselves to the same hypothetical center while extending outwardly, infinitely, at the speed of light.

In the same way, different religious traditions are also oriented to the same center and source by virtue of nothing more than their existence. They occupy, extend, and overlap in the same time and space. Now, with dramatic global and cultural communication, their overlaps and occupation of common space become undeniable. The former luxury of splendid isolation is no longer possible.

Concentric spiritual pathways circumnavigate the same center even as they perceive the other in separate space. That, however, is an illusion. In actuality, they are composed of the same energy and are oriented to the same source. Form and position, as related to the center, is the only difference between them, and that is a relative difference. Generally speaking, that form and position is what preoccupies people in the world of comparative religion. The answers we seek, however, are found beyond form and position.

The domain of the sacred is massive, an unfathomable network of concentric circles composed of the same energy infinitely extending outward from the center. And the circle is the keeper of this mystery, holding the tension between what is stable and what is unfolding within it.

If a person is to follow the particular path of one of the great religious traditions, it will require just that, following a path to a time-honored and spirit-centered end. In that regard, the spiritual journey *is* like a path that leads up the mountain, climbs the ladder, or circles the holy obelisk.

When it comes to defining the relationship of one tradition to another, however, the first recognition must be that all this path-finding takes place on one band of circumference among the many concentric circles. All of these bands are oriented to a shared center, a universal dynamic more determinative than their distinctive location. This is what the theologian Paul Tillich referred to as the *God beyond God*.[1]

If God is simply one being alongside other beings, that remains a contingent construct of our subjective understanding, a relative portrait of an absolute reality. All descriptions, even as comprehensive as they might seem to us, are inevitably partial and incomplete. This does not mean the answer is to cobble together partial pictures to assemble the whole, like borrowing pieces from disparate places in order to complete an entire puzzle. It goes beyond that.

There is always a God beyond our concept of God because our concept of God is a finite view within infinity, always existing on one circumference of the infinite network of concentric circles. At the center is the God beyond God, beyond knowing, transcendent, defying both control and description. It is to this ultimate source that we all are tethered. It is to this that all the

1. Tillich, *Courage to Be*, 190.

great traditions point, knowingly or unknowingly, incompletely, with differing degrees of intensity or richness.

God cannot be understood, ultimately, as one object among others, even as a superlative being, and still remain the source, the center of all beings. The multiple arcs of vast concentric circles are home to our relative understandings. They circle and are related to the one center, the one source that is neither created nor relative, to which everything else is oriented and derives its being.

This is the real basis for interfaith discussion and relationship: the vast circle of the cosmos, its multi-faceted rainbows and one center.

God is One, unified, and infinite, the Center of the Circle. And the $\sqrt{\text{God}} = \text{God}$ every time.

3

A Piece of Pi

IF YOU NEED TO unlock the circle in front of you, π is your go-to boy. You'll recognize him by his nametag. Sometimes it says 22/7 and other times 3.14. They are pretty much interchangeable, and which one he wears depends on the day and his mood. If you drive by his house, you'll see people standing on the front porch, waiting, holding bags full of all kinds of circles. Everyone knows that π is tight with the circle; there's no measuring a circle without him. Without him you're not going to be able to multiply the diameter to find the circumference. Nor can you begin to determine the area of the whole circle because you need π multiplied by the radius squared.

But he's also a mystery man, often seen wearing sunglasses, even at night. He can never be entirely defined or known since his integers extend out infinitely. But his mojo works anyway. That's all that matters. You don't know exactly how, but it does. So you have to accept the mystery that comes along with the key. π unlocks the circle all right, but you don't exactly know the one doing the opening. Not completely, you don't. The partially known reveals the hidden. In the end, concentric circles share not only the same center, but π itself.

When it comes to the spiritual realm, it's all about keys and mysteries, too. Disclosed paths lead to certain doors which are accessed by certain keys that open particular rooms that connect to other dimensions. And religious traditions offer such keys, sign markers that take their adherents on a strange journey toward the mystery.

A general spiritual awareness, a vague sense of the cosmic power grid, might inspire awe, but not provide a meangingful way to make sense of it. That's why religious traditions develop in the first place, in order to differentiate, guide, provide a particular path, and live in a purposeful relationship with the mystery.

When it comes to the Christian path, the role and function of π is just about as analogically parallel to the identity of Christ as you're going to get. He provides a distinctive key to unlock the mystery of the circle of God. Because the key belongs to the lock and the lock opens with the key, the key participates in, is a part of, and belongs to the same mystery which it opens. Christ participates fully in the nature of that which he helps to unlock. That's what the Messiah does; the announcer becomes part and parcel of what is announced.

As Kathryn Tanner puts it, Christ provides "a clue to the pattern or structure that organizes the whole even while God's ways remain ultimately beyond our grasp."[1]

AΩ

In the land of theoretical physics, those searching for a unitary theory of everything have always been puzzled by the missing pieces. Quantum reality occurs at the sub-atomic level, with the elegant dynamics of the smallest of units of energy, particles. Why is it, physicists continue to ask, that these sub-atomic particles actually coalesce to form what we know as mass? If they are so resistant to clumping together, why do they? Why is there any solid form of energy at all? What slows these particles down in their course?

1. Tanner, *Christ the Key*, viii.

One answer to this conundrum has been the hypothetical *Higgs field*, a sticky energy field that causes particles to clump. And now with extensive testing with proton collisions at near the speed of light, it has become much more than hypothesis; it has become theory. The Higgs particle, popularly called the "God Particle," has been identified as the singular missing link to the explanation of how energy becomes matter. It allows energy to manifest in mass. The Higgs particle is the particle that determines much of the behavior of other particles. It is at once the explanation for the way that other particles slow and clump, and how energy transforms into matter.

In the Christian tradition we speak in terms of the creative wisdom and purpose of God that manifests in the created order. Christians embrace the mystery of the transcendent mind of God, the Word, manifesting in matter, in the flesh, in the personhood of Jesus. The Word becomes flesh. Energy becomes matter.

In the same way that the Higgs particle provides an explanation for how energy and matter relate without disclosing how or why it exists in the first place, so the key of Christ doesn't disclose everything behind the door. We have to walk through it without certainty. And the one who walks through has to be open to being unlocked, too.

We cannot get to the bottom of π anymore than we can know why the Higgs particle is there in the first place. Neither can we fully plumb the mystery of Christ. But we do have enough to unlock the mystery of the circle, as least as much as any mortal can. The mystery of Christ leads to the hidden God of Christ. The greater our circle of knowledge, the greater the surface of what we don't know.

Christ is the key that opens the lock, π that opens the circle. This includes the Jesus of history, his life, teaching, and eventual suffering for the sake of loving God and humanity, and also the Christ that transcends history, the continuity of Messiah in the life of God and the world. And though they are distinct, the Jesus of history and the Christ of faith, they have a continuity that, received by faith, creates a transforming reality.

AΩ

To embrace a Christian view of the world we need to hold two things at the same time. The first is that everything is an expression of the Oneness of God. The second is the distinctive role of Christ in understanding that one reality. For the Christian way, both are necessary.

The Oneness of God is indivisible. The reality of God and the cosmos is a unified singularity. Everything that exists flows from that existence. At the same time, Christians make a faith claim that is married to this Oneness: The One God was manifested in time and space in Jesus of Nazareth. As the Apostle Paul reminded us, this historical particularity has been a stumbling block for many, especially those who cannot comprehend the earthiness of God's action. What appears weak and foolish is actually the power and wisdom of God (1 Cor 1:22–25). This paradox has been called the *scandal of particularity*. And it has scandalized many.

When the One God acts in particularity, emerges in time and space, fills it to overflowing, that does *not* mean that the One God is absent from every other time and place, as though the One God is *limited* to particular time and space. God did not leave one geographic place and relocate to another as our human bodies do. That relocation idea is the product of a classical theism, with supernatural beings moving from here to there.

To the contrary, God is present everywhere in everything in every moment. Within this ubiquitous web of sacred energy, points of intensity emerge. These are holy anomalies in the web of time and space where novelty and intensity join to make a particular impact. That novel impact does not in the slightest way reduce or diminish the universal Oneness of God. Rather, the part always belongs to and points to the whole. Just because a comet comes crashing to the earth it does not mean that, say, the laws of gravity are suspended; they are not. The anomaly does not alter the preexisting reality. Jesus may emerge up and out of the web of history, but he does not alter the primary forces of the One God in place. His appearance transforms all those captured by his revelation of what already is. π never diminishes or replaces the circle, but instead unlocks its mystery, leading to revolutionary understanding and transformed connection.

In addition, though π is directly related to the circle by its constitution and purpose, it retains its own novelty, identity and particularity. It still retains its qualitative identity of 3.14. The circle does not diminish its infinite identity sequence, but instead completes and fulfils it. The novelty of Jesus' humanity was not replaced by the universality of the One God. His distinct humanity, his 3.14, was fulfilled and brought to the height of its potential as a particular revelation of the One God in time and space. Christ is π, the one who unlocks the dimensions of the circle of which he is a part. And that is the power and wisdom of God.

AΩ

Christ, our π, provides a double-sided significance, one that preoccupied the early theologians of the Church (Chalcedon, 451 C.E.). The figure of Christ is taken to be a normative paradigm of *what humanity can be*, but at the same time a paradigm of *what God is*. It is both of these; π unlocks the circle of God and the circle of humanity. In the same way that speaking of π is to simultaneously speak of the circle, so to speak of Christ is to at once speak of God and humanity.

As Christ our π reveals, reflects, embodies, and fulfills the Oneness of God, so we know something in particular about the nature of God.

Christ reveals what is hidden

"No one has ever seen God; the only son, who is in the bosom of the Father, he has made him known." (John 1:18)

Christ makes known the infinite under the conditions of finitude. That takes place in at least two ways.

As the revealer, Christ is tapped into the energy source, making it available to those tapped into him. In addition, Christ acts as a funnel through which the knowledge of God is accessed as it is contained, directed, and focused. For example, if I try to access the power of electricity directly, such as putting my finger in the electric outlet, the result is less than pleasant. The flow is too much, and, considering my limits, I can't make use of it in any helpful way. I am not equipped for it. But plug in an adaptor, a device that modulates the current, then that same current powers my laptop.

If I am wondering how I might connect with a universe that seems big and impersonal, a reality too big to embrace, then I reach to a place where I can, to the revealer. Once I may have felt alienated and estranged from my source, but through him I am brought near. I am reconciled to the ineffable mystery of the circle through π (2 Cor 5:19f) I once was disconnected, but no longer.

One of the great mysteries of deep divine love is that it suffers for the beloved. That means that the source and creator never rests until the whole creation is brought home, in harmony. Because the divine love is not impassive, remote, and removed, but rather involved and participatory, every relationship in the divine economy matters.

As we witness the wild, passionate love of Jesus suffering for his God and his people, we know everything we need to know about love and really everything we need to know about God. Some people are virtuous enough to die for a friend, but the holy love is not based on who is likable and worth saving. The sacred threads of love weave through every created being and each one is worth dying for. Love goes the distance.

If you listen carefully, you can hear the sacred sound track playing in the background. The song is sweet and sad and never ending. It tells of a lover who never gives up on the wandering beloved, always keeping a candle in the window. It's the kind of a song that will break your heart if you let it. What you hear in these sacred lyrics is not only something about the wild-eyed lover who keeps waiting. The notes have also made their way into that inner safe room where you store your deepest regrets, failed hopes, and profound brokenness. The song of a broken-hearted lover reaches in and grabs your broken heart. You *are* the locked circle waiting to be opened. And the one who carries our grief and sorrows is the key.

Christ reflects the radiance

"*He is the image of the invisible God.*" (Col 1:15)

I write these words during a full moon, in a place with very little light pollution, the night full of its own darkness and its own light. The lesser light that rules the night is on parade, full and luminous and close enough to touch. No artificial light is needed as I walk through a small clearing that is surrounded by bordering trees.

Earlier in the day, the greater light, the sun, bore down upon our parched little world with its unrivaled brightness and heat. With clouds on hiatus, nothing stood between me and the big fire in the sky. They say that someday it will meet a cataclysmic end before it collapses in upon itself, the neighborhood of its planets following suit. The earth will be no more. And even if the moon *was* around, we couldn't see it anymore. A mirror isn't a mirror without something to reflect.

When we gaze upon the image of Christ, we see a reflection, and it is not unlike that of the moon. We can say that the moon has its own light, and it seems that way. But even as I was mesmerized by its light in my nighttime walk through the forest clearing, I knew there was a hidden power behind the throne, hiding on the other side of my planet.

The speed of light is constant in a vacuum, 186,282 miles per second (299,792,458 meters per second), and decreases slightly as it refracts through transparent material such as air. Light travels from sun to earth in 8.3 minutes. From moon to earth the time is predictably a fraction of that, 1.3 seconds. Because the speed of light is finite, distance determines the time it takes for it to travel.

The light that reflects off the surface of the moon and travels to earth is traveling at exactly the same speed as light traveling directly from sun to earth, because the speed of light is always constant, regardless of its source. Qualitatively speaking, we receive the same light from the moon as we do from the sun. Then why doesn't the reflected light from the moon light up the night as the sun lights up the day? The sun strikes the surface area of the earth in a distance equal to the earth's diameter. The moon, on the other hand, has a much smaller diameter and a much smaller fraction of that light is passed on. Stars 100,000 light years away from earth are just as big as our own sun, or bigger, but their light is cast in all directions from their spherical surface. We catch a miniscule fraction of the whole. In fact, the farther we are away from the source generating in all directions from a sphere, the smaller portion we receive. The scale of intensity and quantity is much, much less.

So it is with the sun's light reflected on the moon. The intensity is considerably less. It is the same light traveling at the same speed, but a much smaller portion of the entirety makes its way to us.

I remember one time how a very thoughtful young man explained that he was a Christian who really dug Jesus but had great reservations about God. Jesus he got, but God—and all the assumptions that came along with that word—made him much less certain. Is it possible to be a Jesus person and remain quite undecided about God?

On the surface, that point of view might seem backwards. After all, God is the first term and Jesus the second, right? How can you embrace the son of something you question so? It doesn't make any sense. Well, it might not unless you begin to consider it according to light and reflection.

If Jesus is, as Colossians claims, a reflection of something hidden, like the moon reflecting light from a sun beyond our night time horizon, we experience the same light from a much closer vantage point and in an intensity that is palatable. Staring into the sun will blind you. You might begin howling if you stare at the full moon too long, but you won't lose your sight!

When Moses came down from Mount Sinai following his encounter with the holiness of God (Exod 34:29–35), the Biblical narrative says that his face so reflected the glory of God as he taught the people that it shone. After sharing his experience he would veil this radiance from ordinary interactions. This protecting of the glory is in deference to the power of the sacred reality.

The glory of God is pushed down into the marrow of the world and, like the radiance in Moses' face, reflects the hidden realms from whence it has come. We find the glory of God hidden in the world, manifesting itself in our realm of existence. And Christians say that Jesus was similar to Moses, reflecting the holiness to which he belonged and from which he came. Jesus was the moon, close at hand, reflecting the sun's light, its intensity reduced for human consumption.

Whether the sun is too bright for anyone to behold directly or simply hidden from sight, over the horizon of night, the moon provides a reflection of its source. And in Jesus we find the image of the invisible God.

Whether the beginning point for my young friend is God and he then has to figure out how Jesus fits, or it is Jesus and he has to backtrack to the source from there, he is still experiencing the same light traveling at the same speed. The Jesus he embraces is a reflection, to be sure. But that reflection is a refraction of light from its original source. And light is light.

Christ embodies sacred wisdom

"In the beginning was the Logos, and the Logos was with God . . . "
(John 1:1)

In the collection of Hebrew wisdom literature, wisdom is personified as a feminine manifestation of God. She builds her house, prepares a feast, and sends out maids far and wide to invite the simple-minded to share her table: "Come, eat of my bread and drink of the wine I have mixed. Leave simplemindedness and live, and walk in the way of insight." (Prov 9:1–6)

The role of Lady Wisdom is to persuade humanity to leave the ways of folly and join the way that leads to righteousness and peace. It is not an easy job. Human proclivity to self-interest and distortion of the divine imprint is strong. The sheep wander from their fold, often into peril. But Wisdom marks the path toward the truly good life. Wisdom is revealed in pithy sayings and world-jarring parables. Contemplation of her truths leads the open soul toward the God for whom they hunger.

For the faithful Jew this meant fidelity to Torah, the teaching and interpretation of which became the essential way to walk the path. Wise sages and careful scholars spent lifetimes trusting Wisdom to lead them toward the God who had made them his own, giving a law and a land for their flourishing. Prophets arose to speak a timely word of truth and challenge to those who turned from this way, calling for repentance and announcing healing, hope, and restoration. The Messiah would, finally, complete this work, bringing about the repair of the world and the rebuilding of the reign of God on earth.

When Jesus entered the world stage he also called God's people to fidelity to the spirit and intent of Torah. He often spoke as bold prophet, critiquing beliefs and practices that led to spiritual death. His proclamation was linked with healing and casting out the spirits that possessed people and took them captive.

Jesus was also a teacher of unconventional, sometimes shocking wisdom. His favorite theme was the kingdom, realm or reign of God, a divine province that was present, yet on the way, too. The discerning had only to scratch beneath the surface to find it, hiding all along.

Jesus described this sacred reality in terms familiar to wisdom, peppered with sayings and parables. The realm of God is like a farmer watching the miracle of growth, a woman who lost a coin and then found it in joy, a father whose loving kindness outlasted the self-centeredness of a wandering son, and a king who invited the poor and lame to his banquet when others made themselves unavailable. The kingdom of God is like something disgusting that won't go away, but instead takes over the whole place—like corrupting yeast that rots to do its work or a mustard weed that cannot be eradicated. With such evocative language Jesus cast the vision of a different world of God.

He was also the master of short aphorisms, one-liners, zingers that left a sting. When asked why his disciples were not fasting like other dutiful disciples, he parried, "Can the wedding guests fast while the bridegroom is with them?"(Mark 2:26) Describing the ways the spirit creates new spiritual pathways, he said, "No one puts new wine in old wineskins." (Mark 2:22) And to remind his followers of the cost for pursuing this strange kingdom, he said, "Whoever would save his life will lose it, and whoever loses his life for my sake will find it." (Mark 8:35)

In his proclamation, Jesus contrasted the popular wisdom of his day with a shocking one. Like Lady Wisdom in Proverbs, Jesus set a table and invited the simple-minded to eat with him, embracing the higher truth. In the Christian scriptures, the Greek word behind the English wisdom is *Sophia*—also a feminine personification. It was certainly in the spirit of that deep wisdom tradition that Jesus conducted his entire ministry.

In the Christian story, the keeper of the keys also becomes the key himself. The teacher of alternative wisdom becomes that wisdom. Like Lady Wisdom who personifies what she carries, Jesus became identified with the wisdom of God he had always described. For Christians, this is a crucial connection. The proclaimer becomes the proclaimed. The teacher of wisdom becomes wisdom personified. Christ is π by virtue of what is taught, but also because of who he becomes, wisdom writ large.

Hence his identification with the idea of the Logos, the creating wisdom of God that connects with the world (John 1:1). In the prologue to John's Gospel, the gospel writer employed a pre-existing hymn that sang the praises of the Logos. Found in the Greek philosophical tradition, the Logos represented an intermediary force that bridges the gap between pure being and the created order of matter. To say that Christ was the Logos was to identify him as filling a similar role and purpose, a creative bridge between heaven and earth. Wisdom was impossibly pushed down into the world through Christ, who brought wisdom and was himself the embodied wisdom and power of God. To say that he was with God and a part of God is to honor the Oneness formula shared earlier:

$$1\infty = 1\infty + \text{Logos}$$

Christ fulfills the depths of love

As Christ our π reveals, reflects, embodies, and fulfills the One-ness of God, we know something normative about human nature, where the fundamental problems of existence reside, and what we may become. "If anyone is in Christ, he is a new creation." (2 Cor 5:17) This new creation exists by virtue of a one-to-one correlation with the essence of love. In fact, one may only know God through love and without love there is no true knowledge of God at all (1 John 4:7–8).

Soren Kierkegaard located the origin of love in the nature of God itself, however hidden it might be.[2] And if it is hidden in God, it is also hidden in the human heart, like a spring whose source eludes us, even when we hear our nearness to it.

The faithful soul is guided by Jesus' identification of the two greatest commandments, to love God with all one's being and the neighbor as one's self (Matt 22:38–39). Kierkegaard broke the command to love into its component parts: *You shall love.* The command is personal and specific—it is *you* who shall love and not another. The command is imperative, not optional—you *shall* love. And the thing you shall be doing is *loving* and not something else; not primarily experiencing a feeling, but pursuing an action based on the highest possible good for the other.

Christ is π by virtue of fulfilling the reality of love. Christ reveals the hidden nature of the divine love by reflecting it and leading others toward it. The beginning and end of the mystery that unlocks the mystery of God is love; there is no understanding it any other way. π reveals the mystery of the circle of God through its own nature, the nature of love, the only way it may be unlocked.

In one of the congregations I was privileged to serve, an older widow had become gravely ill. Day by day she worsened and no combination of medical care or spiritual practice seemed able to change that trajectory. Most of us simply accepted the inevitability of her demise. We had seen it many times before, that the time of her death had come.

2. Kierkegaard, *Works of Love,* 26.

Then one day we rose to the terrible news that both her son and daughter-in-law had been suddenly killed in a car accident. It was terribly sad and tragic. We questioned whether this woman would even be able to attend the funeral. But it soon became apparent that attending the funeral was the least of her concerns. Beyond her immediate grief loomed something of much greater importance. The deceased parents had left behind two young children, her grandchildren. There was no one else who could care for them. What happened next shocked all of us.

This woman rose from her death bed, bathed, ate, dressed, and cleaned her house. She prepared a room and then took her grandchildren into her own home and proceeded to care for them. This included everything a parent would do for a child. She raised these children until they both graduated from high school. In fact, that is exactly what she always said she hoped for, to see them through high school. If she could do that, she would be at peace. And after high school graduation and the grandchildren were launched out into the world, she went back to her death bed and in a number of weeks went to her rest.

Like many people of faith and those vested with religious leadership, I have read many a book and heard numerous lectures and presentations on a broad spectrum of philosophical and theological concerns. I have written about them. People ask me about such matters and we share extensive discussions. In all of that I cannot remember one thing that has held greater impact for me than the love of this grandmother for her grandchildren. It recast the meaning of divine and human love, its power and purpose, the way love transforms the lover and those who are loved.

If there is any answer to the conundrum of life, it will have to include this dimension. By necessity, the power of love serves as the key to understanding everything else. Jesus was right, after all, that the two greatest commandments revolve around love. God is love, and nothing can really be known about God apart from that. And the absence of love contributes to every human conflict, harm, and estrangement. This is not the stuff of sentimentality. No, it has to do with people rising up off their death beds.

That is precisely why we must insist, however paradoxical it may seem, that love is the primary force at work in the death of Jesus. On the surface of that event much hatred is on display. The Roman system crushed all opposition. Religious authorities came into conflict. Individuals fell downward into the inferior aspects of their human nature. That is all included in the Christian story, one that does not minimize the absence of love, an absence that sets the tragic backdrop for holy light to shine.

Everything that led Jesus to empty himself, to trudge toward the cross, was the product of a lover's heart for the beloved. The God who created and creates out of love was active in Jesus the lover. His passion put him in the line of fire and he took the bullet, like a parent sheltering children from harm.

There is no shortage of explanations of Jesus' death based on hate rather than love. God has been portrayed as a divine being that required a pound of flesh to rectify the cosmic imbalance of justice and satisfy wrath. Someone had to pay; and a stand-in, Jesus, would do. This is simply not a love-based explanation of Jesus' death and it must be rejected. Sacrificing Jesus to make God feel better is unacceptable.

Rather, the only viable explanation of Jesus' death must be grounded in the love of God for humanity and Jesus' love for God and his neighbor. For the Christ who is our π, everything else is a distortion. The love of Christ is like a grandmother who gave her life for those whom she loved. She died at the right time for them and rose from death on account of them. And Jesus did the same. Love changes everything, absolutely everything. It is the key to the lock, what π is to the circle.

God is One, unified and infinite, the Center of the Circle, unlocked with Christ our π, who reveals, reflects, embodies, and fulfills this in love. And the $\sqrt{\text{God}}$ = God every time.

4

Shape Beneath the Shape

*The universe is written in the language of math-
ematics, and its characters are triangles, circles,
and other geometric figures.*

—GALILEO

Art is a lie that makes us realize the truth.

—PABLO PICASSO

In many ancient cultures, geometric shapes were not only understood to comprise the building blocks of the physical world, but to
serve a parallel artistic purpose as well. Though this might immediately draw our minds to the art and architecture of the Egyptians
and Greeks, it is certainly not limited to them. All cultures, East
and West, demonstrated fascination with the language of shape.

During the flowering of the Renaissance, creators such as
Leonardo da Vinci, Piero della Francesca, and Albrecht Dürer

drew extensively on mathematical and geometric principles to both interpret and create their art. Geometry comprised the stuff of life, and art was meant to reflect and represent that.

During the height of *impressionism* people like Manet, Monet and Renoir were preoccupied with the glimmering *surface* of sensation, the compelling interplay of light and color. In time, however, Paul Cezanne led the pack away from that, in another direction, as he slowly and surely came to see and paint the elemental shapes *beneath* the surface. His influence, more than any other, led the way into *post-impressionism*, as the role of geometric shape became conspicuous in artists such as Salvador Dali and Paul Klee.

All of these artists knew, in one way or another, that the world is made of shapes and the interrelationships between those shapes. The interplay of lines, circles, squares, triangles, and multiple combinations thereof are essential to understanding the structure of the universe as we observe it.

At the beginning of the twentieth century, just as mathematics was beginning to make gigantic shifts, a revolution was taking place in portions of the art world. As artists like Georges Braque and Pablo Picasso began to deconstruct the appearance of objects in order to expose their underlying and essential form, *Analytic Cubism* was born. In part, theirs was a reaction against pure realism, representing life as one might with a photograph.

Increasingly, they made explicit the underlying geometric shapes, and as a result, the interior geometric skeleton moved to the exterior. It might be fair to say that their art developed an *exoskeleton*, as with the outer shell of some biological creatures. In architecture, this would be reflected in a move to externalize the structural skeleton. Exposed beams, trusses, and support bars became art, valued for their beautiful and harmonious function, as the ribs were positioned outside the skin.

In the same way, Pablo Picasso deconstructed objects not only to understand them better, but to bring forward the underlying skeleton of geometric shapes as the subject itself. By depicting "normal" reality in these terms, he distorted what is seen while at the same time revealing why it is the way it is. The distortion reveals the truth. Or, put differently, the underlying truth of a thing disrupts how we are accustomed to seeing it.

This path of this artistic revolution was paradoxical. Like Descartes and the positivists, it deconstructed reality, dissecting the whole into its components. But the way and reasons it *reassembled* those components was strikingly different, often bizarre. From the stuff of the old world a new one was created.

Like the smaller above-water portion of an iceberg alerts us to its hidden and much larger underwater mass, the reflective surface of reality both conceals and signals its hidden totality. What we generally observe first is an entity's form. It is only later we come to know something of its deeper function and purpose.

Think of how that applies to physics. Every physical object in the universe is composed of matter which is really a form of energy. But it is the matter and its form that is observed first, rather than the properties which constitute that matter.

As far as the way we know things, this is a primary distinction between Newtonian and Quantum physics. Newtonian physics, for example, regards a pool table with an everyday perception, a common sense observation of velocity, gravity, action-reaction, the transfer of energy, and all the other primary forces. However true those laws are on the surface level, they do not begin to take account of the unseen dynamics, those that exist on the Quantum level, an unseen world existing on the atomic and sub-atomic level. You are not aware of that when you watch the eight ball drop into the corner pocket. The deeper level of existence requires deeper methods of investigation. There is shape beneath the shape; and whether in geometry, art or physics, the unseen determines the seen more than can be imagined.

AΩ

From the standpoint of faith, perhaps no other theologian has drawn together the aims of faith with those of art quite like Jacques Maritain. As one living in close proximity to artistic modernism, he provided a theological basis for understanding the creative process. That basis included a Christian worldview and the fundamental notion that everything is *unfinished*. The artist is compelled to complete that unfinished picture.

Maritain knew that modernism in the early twentieth century was moving toward exposing the inner structure of reality rather than simply representing its appearance. The faithful artist, he insisted, should be about exposing what is already given, however hidden it might be. That exposure would require seeing every imaginable combination of the buried raw stuff of the world, and, once seen, reshaping and re-presenting it.

The artist of integrity, said Maritain, must avoid simply presenting that which is pleasing, as a purveyor of products to a consumer. Rather, beauty of an honest sort will emerge as a byproduct of artistic integrity. The one who beholds the artist's creation may or may not know why it is so compelling. That is because it is based on something deep, not automatically apparent. In this sense the artist is a contemplator of reality, a truth teller, and revealer of that which is not already known, or perhaps known only intuitively. [1]

So, too, the navigator of the sacred realm discovers a God already there, immanent, yet not fully disclosed or revealed. Faith believes that God is knowable, but only in part, accessible by finite minds as they search out the infinite. In that sense the authentic religious enterprise is a process of uncovering what is there and striving to complete or finish it, at least as far as finishing by finite minds is possible.

A parallel also exists with the depth psychology that emerged in the early twentieth century. The psychoanalysis of the Freudian school and analytical psychology of the Jungian school both plumbed the depths beneath the surface of the conscious mind. For Freud it was unearthing the repressed contents of the personal subconscious. In Jung's case the subconscious held not only personal contents but transpersonal or collective contents, universal symbols, and structures shared by all minds in a common deep well. Regardless, both schools presented the subconscious as highly symbolized. And the interpretation of the symbolic content allowed access to the deep layers of consciousness it represented.

1. Williams, *Grace and Necessity,* 14–22.

The connection of religious consciousness with depth psychology is evident in at least two ways. The first is the recognition that the surface of consciousness is just that, the surface, a layer that conceals something beneath it. What is seen is but part of the picture and the most significant aspect of reality is masked or veiled by our conscious minds.

The second is equally important, namely, that this personal or transpersonal subconscious content is expressed primarily in symbolic terms. The religious person or group insists that, much like the view of dreams or symbols in psychoanalysis, religious stories and universal symbols reveal a deeper layer of consciousness. When the deeper shape beneath the shape is named we experience spiritual epiphanies, the deep calling to the deep (Ps 42:7).

When a mystic contemplates an icon, sings a psalm, or waits in silence, he or she acts on a conviction similar to that held by physicists, artists, psychoanalysts, mathematicians, and poets; much more resides beneath the apparent surface and what is seen, a substantial unseen domain holding treasures, a deeper story.

That is precisely why religious language is first and foremost the language of symbol, metaphor, poetry, and the stuff of dreams and visions. No one can access these deeper levels without faith and trust, leaping off the ledge of rational proof, just as a physicist or astrophysicist cannot speak of atoms or dark matter with only what the unaided eye provides.

Therefore, Biblical language, like the language of other sacred scriptures, is destroyed by those who rush to literalize it. The language of transcendence points to realities beyond ordinary comprehension, and this requires mythical language, parabolic language, symbolic language, and poetic language. Any project that shrinks these forms into scientific tomes with rational proofs destroys them.

An example of language that bears multi-layered symbolic freight is the use of *double entendres* in the Gospel of John. It is not difficult to see that the entire narrative of John is propelled by words and phrases with dual meanings. Most typically the narrative is constructed with dialogues between the character of

Jesus and "straw people" who set Jesus up to clarify what they have missed, thereby allowing him to reveal deeper significance.

In the story of the encounter with the Samaritan woman (John 4:4–26) Jesus asks the woman for water and she resists—as she is a Samaritan and a woman in public. Jesus informs her that he could give her *living water* (4:10), but she misinterprets his meaning and asks for a way to have a source of water that never runs dry. By missing the point, she allows the character of Jesus to clarify and restate the other side of the double entendre—namely, that there is a water of a spiritual nature that rushes up like geyser from the inside (4:14). That is not the end of her lack of comprehension, however, which allows Jesus to lead us, the readers, to deeper and deeper levels of truth beneath the surface.

When the Jewish Kabbalah presents the Tree of Life, based on the Biblical narrative from Genesis (2:9), it does so in a transformed state, as a mystical symbol. The symbolic tree is laden with the attributes of God, the *sephirot*, in their masculine, feminine, and neutral forms. As an esoteric symbol, the Tree of Life is not simply a tree; it transports those who contemplate its multi-layered truth to the source of those truths, the root of every attribute, the shape beneath the shape, the energy beyond form and matter.

In every case the hidden dimension of the holy, accessed through symbol and story, is revealed, unmasked and unveiled, filling us with wonder and awe.

It was Douglas Hofstadter who comprehensively analyzed the deep patterns in mathematics, art, and music and found that they all functioned in the same way. What he found were deep loops and patterns that lived under the surface of almost everything, and these strange loops and patterns create tensions at the intersection of the finite and infinite. They are always laden with a strong sense of paradox.

The mathematician Gödel developed an *Incompleteness Theorem* in which "all axioms include undecidable propositions." [2] Neither a complete system nor absolute boundaries exist, no matter how comprehensive the propositions. Nothing can exhaust the

2. Hofstadter, *Gödel, Escher, Bach*, 6

complexity. The implication is, of course, that as every mathematical system establishes its own parameters, it simultaneously limits itself. That process necessarily limits access to infinite possibilities.

The artist M.C. Escher created his art with recursive patterns, paradoxical patterns within patterns. This allowed the finite and infinite to do the impossible, to merge, allowing finite patterns to unfold infinitely. Like boxes nested inside boxes, his patterns—often rationally impossible—extend forever.

The recursive patterns of twentieth century art, however, are not unknown to the history of art or the fabric of nature itself. Islamic geometric or scripture art, often circling the inside of mosques, accomplishes the same feat; a finite space is wrapped in unfolding, infinite patterns. Continuing and unending Celtic knots and weaves add another dimension of reality as they overlay such finite spaces as illuminated manuscripts and high crosses. The self-consuming snake, the *Uroboros*, is a complete loop, creating paradox by means of a pattern that has a beginning and ending, yet no beginning and ending. It is at once finite and infinite.

If these ancient artists intuitively mirrored the recursive patterns of nature observable to the eye, they did not have access to what we have now. They came to their conclusions without the knowledge of replicating fractals on the micro and macro levels, the elegant and intricate symmetry of the strands of DNA, or the way that the complex biological or social systems often contain their own self-organizing mechanisms.

Music also contains strong parallels to the infinitely extending patterns of mathematics and art. When it comes to the form and motion of music, the *fugue* is the most conspicuous of recurring patterns. And as regards fugues, J.S. Bach is the undisputed master.

A fugue is a set of variations, sequences of a stated theme which make staggered entrances in different tonal ranges. It is always self-referential; it unfolds in growing complexity even as it always remains true to itself. And it would be possible, if time were unlimited, to extend those patterns and entrances indefinitely.

Considered together, the musical patterns of the fugue, the artistic expression of repeating patterns, and infinitely extending mathematical sets all express the same reality in different terms: there are deep patterns embedded in the structure of life, unfolding, replicating, and determining the shape of the surface above them. The shape beneath the shape is positioned somewhere between the rational and irrational, finite and infinite, structural and novel.

Cinema provides another language of our culture that reveals deep loops and patterns. Film both presents and interprets reality, and filmmakers often stand on the edge of cultural fault lines. Three examples immediately come to mind.

The Matrix presents an illusory virtual world in which redemption comes by exposing the fabricated digital curtain of reality and how we are controlled by it. Messianic figures fight for the truth beyond the deception. Liberation comes only when believed illusion is unmasked.

Inception plays with multiple layers of the unconscious mind, navigating these levels as one would traverse different sets of the same play. Each level is connected to the next, though separated by a membrane of time, and accessed by traveling through dream states.

The Life of Pi recognizes that reality and its essence may be represented variously, either through historical facts or in a wildly imaginative and symbolized allegory. Both may represent the outlines of the same history but interpret its meaning quite differently.

Though the purposes may be different, contemporary cinema often has the same impact that ancient oral storytelling and evocative literary traditions once did: story is presented, meaning suggested, morals reinforced, hidden aspects surfaced. In the case of multi-layered films of transcendence, the audience is transported from one layer or dimension of reality to another. In film today, sensory experience can be highly manipulated to appear both realistic and surrealistic at the same time. The perceptual awareness of the viewer may seem dream-like as stories are wrapped inside other stories and time shifts quickly from past to present to future.

The Bible is just such a book as this, of another genre, laced with transcendent meanings. Ancient audiences read and listened with much the same interest as movie audiences approach the latest film release today. Children of the Enlightenment do not often approach the reading of scripture in this same dramatic way. We are inclined to read and study it as a canon of documents, sacred history and its lists of morals, all systematized, harmonized, sanitized, and domesticated. Fortunately for us, our children often save us from this fate. Upon hearing impossible words of Biblical stories, they often stare wide-eyed, gasping with shock and wonder. The Bible may not be *The Lion King*, but it could come close.

Consider how the apostle Paul made his argument for the resurrection, both of Jesus and also for Christian existence. He did so by employing an evocative metaphor of comparison between the grain of wheat that must die and change form, and our physical and spiritual bodies (1 Cor 15:35–50). Spirit and flesh are of two orders, an observation that does imply self-deprecation of the body. It rather refers to different planes of existence. One dimension is found on the surface, material existence. The other emerges as a seed does, transforming through death, breaking through and plunging under. Resurrection operates in a similar way, by transforming existence by what's under its surface.

ΑΩ

Plenty of language in the Bible and in our Jewish and Christian traditions refers to God's saving of us. In theology we refer to it as *soteriology*. Far from the popular evangelical use of the term *saved*—moving to a state of spiritual grace—the Bible most typically refers to the way God delivers us. That deliverance comes in many forms. In the most earthy case it refers to delivering us from harm, enemies, disease, and death itself. On the spiritual level salvation may refer to deliverance from ignorance, our sin, or a life without God. We are saved from ourselves, the ways in which our worst inclinations ruin us or violate our neighbor. The idea of salvation, saving, being saved, is ubiquitous in the Biblical narrative: We need help in the worst way. Thank God, help is at hand.

I will be the first to say that I need to be saved from lots of things, including myself, and delivered to another place, a locale different from my self-created prisons. I accept that the power to do so frequently comes from sources beyond me, or at least my conscious self. But what I have not been so clear about is how *God has to be saved first.*

To sharpen the point, the failure of one image or concept of God often necessitates its abandonment. This re-envisioning is imperative in order to save, rescue, and deliver God from oblivion. Certain models and concepts must be discarded because they cease to make any sense. Those images of God must be left behind in order to rescue God. In my case and for countless others, God has to be saved before we are.

This was the gist of the highly misunderstood "death of God" movement of several decades ago. Thinkers such as Gordon Kaufman proposed that the images of God that once carried the sacred freight had ceased to work and were becoming impediments to faith. New images that reflected current understandings of the world would have to take their place. That project of reconstruction is a never-ending one.

The new militant atheism, propelled by such prophets as Richard Dawkins, is primarily a movement that fights against the windmills of classical theism. I understand their battle. They have unsheathed the swords of modernity against classical notions, models and forms of the divine that are no longer tenable. But the new atheism is not so new; those images of God have been dying for a long time. For many the funeral took place long ago. That is why I find the not-so-new atheism such a bore, an old project chewing the same cud. The windmills they courageously assault stand dilapidated on abandoned islands, their blades frozen in place.

Classical theism was largely formed by Semitic and Hellenistic images of a super-being. Its divine images are often based on anthropocentric projections of human qualities or characteristics. That is understandable, of course. How else do we describe the world or what we experience as sacred within in except in terms to which we relate, referents from our own experience? That project, though, was doomed to failure from the beginning. It is impossible for a non-whirlwind to describe a whirlwind. Job encountered that, of course, as he fell silent in his smallness before the ineffable mystery of it all (Job 40:1–5).

The image of a big super-being among lesser ones has now been rendered irrelevant not only by the exploration of outer space, but of inner space. The question, "Where is God?" is the product of a classical theism that locates God here or there. It has now become the question no one is asking.

All of this defines the problem for any human being living in the twenty-first century. Faced with a choice between the God of classical theism or no God, people are choosing the latter, no God, because they cannot believe in the slightest in the God of classical theism. Presented with no other alternatives, they are simply opting out, the baby thrown out with the bath water. The classical God that wields external power, pulls the strings of human existence as a master puppeteer, and demands obedience in order to avoid punishment has been deleted. It was inevitable, only a matter of time.

What has been discarded, though, is not the essence. What has been jettisoned is a particular shape or form on the surface. Many who felt compelled to do the discarding have not discovered another way beneath the surface, a way to the shape beneath the shape. Fortunately, another pathway is available. God may be saved, and therefore we may be, too. And how? By moving from Newton to Quantum.

With a little help from Process Theology and Quantum Physics, we may embrace the deep purposeful power and patterns of the universe, embedded in the creation, co-creating life with an immanent God.

Process thought, developed and articulated by philosopher and mathematician Alfred North Whitehead, has been adapted for theological purposes by such theologians as John Cobb, Charles Hartshorne and David Griffin. A second and third generation of Process Theologians has continued to refine and expand its theological domain and reach. The result includes an understanding of the creating God that participates in the process and unfolding of the universe rather than a coercive being external to it. As such, the active purposeful God is always discovered to be present in the world, beneath its surface, leading and luring all created beings toward unrealized potential in the spirit.

Similarly, Quantum Physics, especially particle physics, recognizes that the real story is always told on the sub-atomic level. In that ordered but seemingly chaotic world beyond ordinary observation, the energy of the universe unfolds, a hidden mystery within everything. For billions of years it has unfolded to this very moment, a massive past leading to those of us who inhabit this tiny continuity within time and space.

Taken together, the insights of Process Theology and Quantum Physics usher us toward a new shape of faith, a new understanding of God and ourselves in the universe. We have moved from Newtonian spirituality to Quantum spirituality. And our models of God shifted as we traveled.

A dynamic spiritual practice consistent with this model of God searches within the unfolding process of life for what is already there: deep, purposeful, and sacred patterns that are immanent, hidden and embedded in the world. The universe is a single gigantic field of pure energy, the body of the divine spirit which is veiled to our knowledge of it. Spiritual apprehension seeks knowledge of and union with this purposeful energy and power, what we have called God.

The goal of spiritual existence, then, is to become one with the source of the universe, to live in harmony with it insofar as it is possible, and to become agents of love, assisting the Spirit to draw all things unto itself. The source of life is found in life itself, everywhere. It is not dualistic, a separate reality that exists over and above life. Like a treasure buried in a field, it is to be found beneath our feet, within all life. However vast and unknowable this reality, we may come to know the whole by encountering even a part of it, a fragment of its complexity. Like the woman who touched the hem of Jesus' garment and experienced the fullness of his power, we touch a part of the great mystery and experience the entirety of what Jesus called the realm of God.

In this quantum orientation to faith, *mystery* emerges as a primary theological category and language of religious experience. Mystery is not only present in the unexplainable; it is sewn into everything known and unknown. It resides alongside all the other five-dollar theological words: creation, incarnation, redemption, holiness, atonement, salvation, wisdom, resurrection, *mystery*. It has become an indispensable part of our religious vocabulary, without which we can barely speak any other word.

The spiritual practices that best compliment a quantum faith and its mystery are uncovering ones; the practice of silence, meditation on icons or symbolic art that point to something beyond them, spiritual reading that discerns meanings beneath the surface of the story, deep encounters with nature, relationships, and suffering that evoke our compassion. What this means is that faith must be understood as more *sacramental* than ever before, with outward and visible signs leading toward an inward and spiritual grace.

A sacramental view of faith is in perfect harmony with a quantum one—namely, that the outside both conceals and reveals the inside. Energy and matter are one, an essence buried in the form, the shape beneath shape. That is not dramatized in any more significant way than through the Christian celebration of the Lord's Supper. When Christians behold the bread and cup of Holy Communion, they at once behold the Christ spirit toward which those symbols point, buried beneath the surface. As the non-canonical Gospel of Thomas puts it, "Split a piece of wood and I am there. Lift up the stone and you will find me there." (77:2–3)[3] It is mystery, of course. But that's the point. It takes us somewhere, to places nothing else can.

God is One, unified and infinite, the Center of the Circle, unlocked with Christ our π, who reveals, reflects, embodies the shape of the mystery beneath the shape of the surface. And the $\sqrt{God}$ = God every time.

---

3. Miller, *The Complete Gospels*, 317.

5

Infinity and Beyond

Of all the questions you might want to ask
about angels, the only one you ever hear
is how many can dance on the head of a pin. . . .
It is designed to make us think in millions,
billions, to make us run out of numbers
and collapse into infinity . . . .

—BILLY COLLINS "QUESTIONS ABOUT ANGELS"

THE MEDIEVAL RIDDLE OF angels on the head of a pin combined two numerical aspects of infinity. The first was that numbers may be added to create an ever growing magnitude; another angel may always be added to the totality and then another. The second was that a geometric shape—the head of a pin—may be repeatedly subdivided into smaller and smaller sub-sets, providing additional but smaller spaces for each added angel.

Provided that angels can become increasingly smaller and fit within the diminishing subdivided space, they can multiply to infinity. This is the case regardless of the original available area— the head of a pin—because it may be subdivided infinitely. If one angel can fit on the head of a pin, an infinite number may as well, provided that the defined space may be subdivided in direct correlation to the number of angels being added.

Our perception of infinity is also shaped by these two aspects, addition and subdividing: the addition or subdividing of infinitely many moments and things in time and space.

AΩ

In the late 1800s and early 1900s, a crisis shook the mathematical world. The German mathematician Georg Cantor developed set theory, the model that included sets of finite and distinctive elements and sub-sets with infinitely many extensions. Up until that time, empiricist mathematicians regarded the notion of infinity as a mathematical taboo, a theoretical impossibility. Such a conjecture as infinity could only take place outside the domain of the measurable. Set theory rocked the mathematical boat, creating new and perplexing possibilities. Does infinity really exist or is it merely an abstraction? And how do philosophical models of thought either help or discourage in its pursuit?

Though the concept of infinity was not unknown to ancients who accepted realities beyond the observable, and was well-developed by philosophers such as Plotinus, who drew a correspondence between God the One and an infinite extension, it was not in favor among the children of the Enlightenment, thinkers such as Comte, Descartes, and Hume. With these positivists there would be no room for the limitlessness of space and time, mystical or non-rational explanations of infinity.

An elite "French Trio" of mathematicians—Emile Borel, Henri Lebesgue, and Rene´ Baire—took on the challenges of set theory, attempting to solve its mysteries *sans* referencing any concepts of infinity. In the end, they crashed into the wall of their own self-limiting theory. Eventually, they all stopped trying. It is well-documented that more than one of them became mentally unstable as a result of attempting to negotiate all the contradictions and paradoxes without the key of infinity to do so.

At the same time, something entirely different was fermenting at Mt. Athos, Greece, in the Pantaleimon Monastery, a center of Russian Orthodoxy for a millenium. With thousands of Russian Orthodox monks in residence, the monastery had become a kind of Russian protectorate. In 1913 Russian ships and troops seized the monastery and deported the monks back to Russia. Why? Because the particular practice of *Name Worshipping* had grown to cause great dissension.

The practice of reciting the *Jesus Prayer* (Lord Jesus Christ, Son of God, have mercy on me) went back at least as far as the desert fathers and mothers of the fourth century. They had taken the Jesus Prayer and created a devotional practice around it, praying it as a repetitive mantra and claiming that the name took them to spiritual union with God. Orthodox opposition attacked such practices as blasphemy; God is always beyond every name of God. The Name Worshippers claimed that any name that refers to the holy participates in that holiness and is a reflection of the holiness to which it points. And so the debate went.

Upon return to Russia, the Name Worshippers went underground. But the thinkers they touched—including the intellectuals and mathematicians—were highly influenced by the movement. Some became practitioners themselves.

One of the central defenders of the Name Worshipper movement was a mathematician-turned-priest by the name of Pavel Florensky. He was a close friend of several leading mathematicians in Russia. One of those friends was Dmitri Egorov, professor of mathematics at Moscow University and the future president of the Moscow Mathematical Society. Egorov would become an influential member of one of the Name Worshipper underground "circles." And an influential student of Egorov was Nikolai Luzin. Together, Pavel Florensky, Dmitri Egorov, and Nikolai Luzin made up the so called "Russian Trio."

As Florensky interpreted the Name Worshipper movement to his intellectual peers—mathematicians, philosophers, and writers— he corrected some of its excesses. For instance, he did not regard the letters making up the names of God as magically endowed. Rather, he understood that naming a reality plunges one into its essence, connects with its power. The practitioners became devoted to the power of symbolism and the way language names reality, the name of God being the most important of all the names.

All of this formed a sharp contrast with the materialism and positivism of the French mathematicians. The Russian movement made a striking and model-shattering connection: *In the same way that the mystery of God is made real by naming it, so the naming of sets in mathematical set theory makes the concept of infinity real.* Suddenly the doorway was open to what had previously been closed: the notion of infinity. The Russians believed that naming creates a reality that was previously inaccessible. And God was perhaps the primary referent by which an unending continuum of infinity might be accessed.

By using this method, the Russians vaulted the perplexities of the new mathematical infinities. In the same way that God was made real by naming God, so infinity was made real by creating names for it. Naming held infinite new possibilities for breakthroughs, a joint venture of religious consciousness and mathematical insight.

Sadly, with the rise of the Communist revolution and its radical materialism, religious insights and concepts were systematically repressed. This repression showed itself not only by liquidating traditional religious communities, but by limiting the kind of thinking that was permitted in academia. Idealists— those who had any notion of something beyond the material level of existence—were rooted out, arrested, charged, tried, disappeared in the Gulag, or executed. The outcome for the Russian Trio and their circle of Name Worshipper peers was no different.

Despite persecution and the conspicuous attempt to silence their voices, it was too late; the earlier breakthroughs and insights of the Russian Trio and the Name Worshipper mathematicians persisted. Ancient wisdom had already circled the dance floor with contemporary thought and left its mark. Naming infinity now allowed for its possibility.

AΩ

Determining the square root of a number requires moving backwards to the original number before it was multiplied by itself. This means that the square and its root are inexorably related to one another, the square always determined by its root. If, therefore, the Oneness of God is always the root of its own square, all manifestations of the oneness of God necessarily refer to the same root. All things extend into the cosmos as the one source multiplied by itself, and all things are the square of that one root.

The oneness and unity of God is the root of all manifestations of God:

$$\sqrt{1} = 1$$

Infinity is at once the root of its own complexity and the square of itself:

$$\sqrt{\infty} = \infty$$

The unity/infinity of God is always the square root of itself:

$$\sqrt{1\infty} = 1\infty$$

In the same way:

$$\sqrt{\text{God}} = \text{God}$$

The center of any circle extends outward with an infinitely long radius and encompasses infinitely many concentric circles. Just as infinitely many numbers exist between any two numbers, so infinitely many concentric circles also exist between any two concentric circles on a radius. All concentric circles share the same relationship of unity with the same center, only differing according to their distance from that same center. Unity and diversity, singularity and multiplicity are included in a seamless divine field.

Like angels on the head of a pin, the integers of π extend out infinitely as a part of the same formula. The magnitude of π is infinite, only a portion of which is required to unlock the mystery of the circle whose concentric rings are also infinite. The key participates in the mystery of that which it unlocks. The mystery of Christ belongs to the mystery of God.

Beneath the surface of reality there exist the primary structures of life, recursive and repeating forms and energies that multiply and replicate infinitely in time and space. The ultimate nature of reality is hidden, disclosed through the eyes of a quantum faith and the insight of physicists, artists, poets and the great religious traditions.

Like the Name Worshippers and Set Theorists, infinity becomes real, becomes viable, once named and defined. By identifying an infinite number of sets that derive from a primary one, unity is translated into infinity. And infinity is the dimension that makes understanding everything else possible.

$$A\Omega$$

Though the book of Job is a wisdom book whose content and style is characteristic of much other literature from the ancient Near East, it also has some similarity in appearance to the Greco-Roman diatribe, a type of classical writing in which viewpoints are presented in a series of speeches. Though Job is not the product of classical writing, we primarily experience its major themes through a dramatic debate, an extended dialogue. The dialogue between Job and his friends, and then between Job and the Lord, expresses the various viewpoints poetically, with passion and immediacy.

The debate centers on a man who, though righteous, has suffered immeasurable loss. Universal questions about suffering surface, and well-meaning friends venture explanations. Though some suffering comes as the direct consequence of our own decisions and behavior, other suffering visits the innocent and is undeserved. Why do the innocent suffer? Is all suffering the result of divine punishment? What explanation, if any, can there be for the seeming randomness of it all? These questions comprise a category that theologians call *theodicy*. And Job is the supreme exemplar of its type.

Against notions that all suffering arises as a punishment for sin, Job makes the powerful argument to the contrary. The real theological problem with suffering is exposed when a person's pain or distress is unrelated to anything they or anyone else has done. Sin may bring suffering, but not all suffering comes as the result of sin. Job makes the case for this perspective most persuasively. But his concerns do not end there.

The most difficult question can only be taken up between Job and his God, a conversation which necessarily places the mortal on shaky moral ground. As Job takes the Lord to task for unfairness, arbitrariness and capriciousness, the table soon turns; Job is the one being cross-examined: "Where were you when I laid earth's foundations?" (Job 38:4) The witnesses in the courtroom look on and listen as the Lord-Prosecutor describes an indescribably long compendium of creation acts, all of which took place without the benefit of Job. He was neither present nor necessary for them to occur. Even if Job had existed at the time, and he did not, his presence would have been unimportant.

When confronted with the weight of this truth, Job is silenced, which gives the book its profundity and enduring mystery. One can wait forever for a conclusive solution to this problem. But no matter your patience, no matter your persistence, no matter your obsessive preoccupation, the answers will not be forthcoming. You, as a mortal, are in no position to judge. The reasons for suffering are simply beyond your comprehension. And that is how the book of Job leaves it—unresolved.

One of the reasons that the book of Job is so powerful is its appeal to unimaginably complex creation within limitless time. The magnitude of scale and unending extension of time contribute to Job's collapse into his new awareness: his smallness of scale and brief span of life. He is a flea that is here today and gone tomorrow, both impotent and fleeting. He knows nothing of a limitless past in which the infinitely many complex creatures were created.

Like a physicist backtracking to the moment of the big bang, Job is awestruck with the immensity of the universe and massive nature of time, something finite minds simply cannot grasp. He has been slain by infinity. And he has been saved by it, too, though he does not know it.

Job stands mute at the edge of infinity. This edge can be approached, but never crossed. The voice of the whirlwind, the voice of infinity, asks where we were when it all began and what we could have done about it even if we were. The implied answer, of course, is nowhere and nothing. Though we may not resist asking such questions, we are not qualified to answer them. Its impossibly dense origins bring us to silence.

AΩ

As Job extends the mystery of God toward an incomprehensibly distant past, the Revelation of John of Patmos does just the opposite; it projects the experience of present hope into an indefinite future. His vision transports the reader toward a transformed reality beyond finite time. At the beginning of the vision of the New Jerusalem we are told, "I am the Alpha and the Omega, the beginning and the end." (Rev 21:6) In other words, the oneness and infinity of God has been and always will be; it existed before we were and will exist after we are. The Alpha and Omega transcend all chronological time. But what is true of time is also true of space.

In the same way that the holy city is transformed by an angel in Ezekiel 40–42, the New Jerusalem of the apocalyptic book of Revelation (21:1—22:2) also undergoes utter transformation: an angel reveals and measures the city's sacred geometry.

The perfect square perimeter (as also found in Ezekiel and the Temple Scroll of the Dead Sea Scrolls) has twelve gates, three per side. In Revelation, however, the city is as high as it is wide and long, making it a gigantic cube (21:16), the picture of balance and internal strength. The repetition of the number twelve reinforces the symbolic wholeness and completeness of the people of God, the tribes, and apostles. The entirety of this sacred shape is adorned with the same jewels that bedazzled the breastplate of the priest Aaron (Exod 28:17–21, 39:10–13), as well as gold and other precious gems. This all communicates the superlative value and holiness of the new heaven and new earth. But perhaps more awe-inspiring than even the perfection of the heavenly symmetry is its unfathomable enormity: the cube is 12,000 stadia wide, long, and high (or 15,000 miles in each dimension).

The combination of this proportion, scale, and material symbolizes infinity within space, an unbounded and unlimited locale. With the sacred unmediated by a temple, light unmediated by sources other than the luminous nature of God, the river of life flowing out from the city to water the world, and the tree of life providing its twelve fruits and many leaves for the healing of the nations, the city is at once infinite and sacred.

Whereas Job confronts us with impossibly dense origins, Revelation draws us toward an incomprehensible unfolding future. In contrast to our present form of existence with its finite boundaries, the new heaven and new earth are unbounded and limitless in both time and space. As with the Name Worshippers and theorists of Set Theory, naming new realities and unbounded potentials allows them to exist, or more precisely, for us to know and accept that they do exist. Naming infinity allows infinity to be what it is for us. It then informs the nature of everything else. Infinity is woven into the fundamental unity of all things.

AΩ

By a very young age the images of God that were presented to me by church or culture began to fade, wane, degrade, and lose their power. As they did, I began to ask why. Was it just me? Or did this dilution of the divine relate more to the constructs that were being served up? These questions sent me on a quest, and that exploration has never ceased.

In relatively short order I began to realize that my discomfort with these presentations of God originated with their simplistic anthropocentrism, a creating of God after the human image. Nothing in my world or perception of it led me to accept these constructs of ultimate truth. That included the customary way in which Jesus was presented.

Though I didn't know it at the time, I was already asking how the images of God we assume jibe with the universe as we perceive it. No one should ask us to adopt a first-century world view to live by faith. And yet that is exactly what much of religious life has expected us to do. That view has included constricted methods of interpreting scripture and conventional assumptions about just what reflected the virtuous life.

It is not only that one of the many streams of Christian tradition asked us to accept something illogical as true or accept on faith that which could not be proved or known. It is not only that the Christian story was presented with internal contradictions as regards the nature of God and purposes of Jesus. No, the real problem was a huge relevancy gap.

The classic presentation of faith described by the church was not in sync with the other forms of knowledge I knew through every other pathway—science, the arts, psychology, mythology, anthropology. They were not in sync until I started listening carefully to thinkers who drew them together in a powerful, synthesized way. They made a strong correlation between the ancient wisdom and contemporary knowledge and experience. More and more the power of symbol and metaphor became a sure pathway to wisdom.

That is why *intersections* became so important to me: intersections between prayer and physics, sexuality and creativity, art and symbols, healing and beauty, ethics and wisdom, spirituality and mathematics. What is there about the mathematical underpinnings of the world that point to its elegance and describe its beauty, even its sacred dimensions? What is there about the mystical insights of faith that elicit a sense of awe, wonder, and hope? And what comes from them when we allow them to speak in concert, on at least parallel tracks, perhaps using different language to describe some of the same things differently?

Insight and a sense of wonder may be obtained from either mystical spiritual apprehension or scientific discoveries of mind-shattering complexity or beauty. This sense of awe may overcome the hard-hitting scientist who stands before the elegant design of the universe and the religious devotee who surrenders the rational to ever deeper layers of consciousness. It is even possible for them to join hands and waltz to that music together. When that happens new insights are born.

When I realized that the contributions of the ancient wisdom and the insights of other sources of knowledge were not oppositional, but rather complementary to one another, a whole new world emerged. This is not a case of either-or. It is not even a case of both-and. This is a seamless, unified, and infinite field, a center with its circles, mystery unlocking mysteries, fundamental form beneath the appearance of reality, one that grows in infinite dimension even as we name it so.

To enter this realm of understanding we must stand with the humility of Job, the wonder of a child, and the curiosity of every seeker who ever dared look toward the future. We are but a grain of sand on the beach of eternity. But eternity presses upon these hearts in infinite ways. There is room for a distinct revelation of this realm through one like Jesus, who becomes the way, the truth, and the life for us. There is also infinite room for the many manifestations of the sacred in the world, of which we are mostly unaware.

All of this leads us, drives us back to the one centermost point of all, the simplest of all, the unity within every complexity, and the pattern beneath every appearance. All is one. We call it God, but you may call it anything you like. It is the most beautiful, elegant, wondrous, unlimited existence within everything that is. It animates all that is animated, the root of every square. Everything is derivative of this One, coming from it and returning to it, the Alpha and Omega, beginning and middle and end. And its infinite future is one with its being, its energy and essence traversing time even as it changes form.

God is One, unified and infinite, the Center of the Circle, unlocked with Christ our π, who reveals, reflects, embodies the shape of the mystery beneath the shape of the surface. And the $\sqrt{God} = God$ every time.

Conclusion

As I worked on organizing the material of this book into a whole, a pattern began to work on me, designing me, as it were. But where did that pattern come from? Was it merely a memory trace, some remembrance of another book, another project, another presentation? Did the pattern come from something already existing in the hardwiring of my brain, a reflection of my network of synapses? Was it some familiar liturgical pattern? Or is it a more ontological matter, a reflection of the way of things are in the universe, subterranean universal patterns?

You may have noticed that the center point chapter of this book is *A Piece of Pi*. That is not accidental, since π serves as the guiding metaphor for Christ. For me Christ stands at the center with as much leading to it as flowing from it.

If you look more carefully you find recursive sets, patterns within patterns:

{Number 1 [Circle < Pi> Shape] Infinity}

A Piece of Pi is the centerpiece, surrounded by pairs that are entangled with one another, such as in particle theory: Chapter 2, *Circle Up*, is entangled with Chapter 4, *Shape Beneath the Shape*; and Chapter 1, *The Number 1*, is entangled with Chapter 5, *Infinity and Beyond*.

Within each set, sub-sets may be added and extend infinitely. Beginning with 1, a singularity, every number includes that singularity and itself, a oneness that is inescapable and is the basis of all complexity, no matter how random or chaotic it might seem. Every point on every radius of a circle is in exactly the same relationship to the center, no matter the distance from the center or resulting intensity or richness. The mystery key that unlocks and understands the area of a circle is Pi, a number to unlock other numbers. Like a Bach fugue, a theme may repeat, with staggered entrances in time and at different frequencies, or levels of reality. Like Escher's recursive art, the set pattern multiplied leads from finite to infinite without losing the distinctiveness of the finite or being limited by it. And the act of naming creates the reality that once seemed inaccessible, infinity.

The end of the matter is the simple but profound truth that $\sqrt{God} = God$. You might attempt to wrestle that formula to the ground until it cries uncle. That would be perfectly understandable. In fact, that may be your starting place. You may have to first engage in intellectual combat before you move on to something else. As you will discover, however, the problem with that approach is that you will be attempting to provide a rational answer to a non-rational question. Perhaps it is best understood as a *koan*. $\sqrt{God} = God$ may need to so rattle the cage of consciousness that it renders your original question irrelevant, causing you to collapse into mystery. If it does, that would be a good thing.

About the Author

TIM CARSON IS A pastor and writer whose works include several books and numerous poems, articles, and essays. His interests include travel, the arts, cinema, scuba diving, and the lore of the Santa Fe Trail. In his spare time you might find him playing the tin whistle or working with birds of prey at a raptor rehabilitation center. He lives in Rocheport, Missouri, and you may follow him at http://vitalwholeness.wordpress.com.

Bibliography

Augustine, Saint. *The Trinity: The Works of St. Augustine*. Translated by Edmund Hill. Brooklyn, NY: New City, 1991.

d'Espagnat, Bernard. *Veiled Reality*. Boulder, CO: Westview, 2003.

Gaustad, Edwin S. *Faith of the Founders: Religion and the New Nation 1776–1826*. Waco, TX: Baylor University Press, 2004.

Graham, Loren, and Jean-Michel Kantor. *Naming Infinity: A True Story of Religious Mysticism and Mathematical Creativity*. Cambridge: Harvard University Press, 2009.

Hofstadter, Douglas. *Gödel, Escher, Bach: An Eternal Golden Braid*. New York: Basic, 1979.

Kierkegaard, Soren. *Works of Love*. San Francisco: Harper Perennial, 2009.

Maimonides, Moses. *Maimonides' 13 Principles of Faith*. http://www.aish.com/sp/ph/48923872.html.

Miller, Robert J., ed. *The Complete Gospels*. Revised and expanded ed. San Francisco: HarperSanFrancisco, 1994.

Priestley, Joseph. *The Theological and Miscellaneous Works of Joseph Priestley*. Nabu, 2011.

Raymo, Chet. *When God Is Gone, Everything Is Holy*. Notre Dame: Sorin, 2008.

Schachter-Shalomi, Zalman. *A Heart Afire*. Philadelphia: The Jewish Publication Society, 2009.

———. *All Breathing Life Adores Your Name*. Santa Fe, NM: Gaon, 2011.

Tanner, Kathryn. *Christ the Key*. Cambridge: Cambridge University Press, 2010.

Tillich, Paul. *The Courage to Be*. New Haven: Yale University Press, 1952.

Whitehead, Alfred North. *The Concept of Nature*. Cambridge: Cambridge University Press, 1920.

Williams, Rowan. *Grace and Necessity: Reflections on Art and Love*. London: Continuum, 2005.

Wittgenstein, Ludwig. *Tractatus Logico-Philosophicus.* Translated by C.K. Ogden. New York: Harcourt Brace, 1922. http://people.umass.edu/ phil335-klement-2/tlp/tlp-ebook.pdf.

———. *Remarks on the Foundations of Mathematics.* Revised ed. Edited by G.H. von Wright, et al. Oxford: Blackwell, 1981.

———. *Philosophical Investigations. 3rd ed.* Translated by G.E.M. Anscombe. Oxford: Blackwell, 1958. http://gormendizer.co.za/wp-content/ uploads/2010/06/Ludwig.Wittgenstein.-.Philosophical.Investigations.pdf.